The Heart of Friendship

The Heart
of Friendship

❧❦❧

Muriel James and Louis M. Savary

HARPER & ROW, PUBLISHERS
New York   Hagerstown
San Francisco
London

THE HEART OF FRIENDSHIP. Copyright © 1976 by Collins Associates Publishing, Inc., New York City. All rights reserved. Printed in the United States of America. No part of this book may be used or reproduced in any manner whatsoever without written permission except in the case of brief quotations embodied in critical articles and reviews. For information address Harper & Row, Publishers, Inc., 10 East 53rd Street, New York, N.Y. 10022. Published simultaneously in Canada by Fitzhenry & Whiteside Limited, Toronto.

FIRST EDITION

Library of Congress Cataloging in Publication Data

James, Muriel.
   The heart of friendship.

   Includes bibliographical references.
   1. Friendship.   I. Savary, Louis M., joint
author.   II. Title.
BJ1533.F8J38 1976   177'.6   74–25702
ISBN 0–06–064117–7

76 77 78 79 10 9 8 7 6 5 4 3 2 1

Don't walk in front of me,
I may not follow.
Don't walk behind me,
I may not lead.
Walk beside me,
And just be my friend.

ALBERT CAMUS

Contents

Preface

We consider friendship to be the most important relationship known to us. Friendship may occur anywhere—within a marriage or family structure, on a job or in a hobby shop, in an institution or a football stadium. The potential for friendship exists wherever people meet.

This book is about the challenge, the joy, the needs, the stress, the art, the process, and the value of friendship. Friendships are different from friends. Friends are people, while friendships refer to relationships. Friendships can have a life of their own, even as people.

This book primarily is about friendships between people in which each person experiences mutual affirmation, acceptance, and freedom. Incidentally, it points to a possible future of friendships with the universe.

We are deeply indebted to our friends for sharing their experiences and insights. We are also indebted to Abraham Maslow, Erich Fromm, Pierre Teilhard de Chardin, Martin Buber and Eric Berne. Their writings expanded our vision, and we have integrated some of their ideas. However, the basic concepts in this book are ours, particularly that of the Third Self.

Naturally, we hope that this book will be read by many, but we had to write it for ourselves even if read only by a few. Hopefully, you are one person who will find it exciting. We've been excited while writing it. We discovered that although we shaped the book, the book—like friendship—has also shaped us.

The true language of friendship is not spoken in words but in heartfelt meanings. It comes from deep within, expressing itself in an intelligence not bound by language or logic.

Friends speak a language of the heart, and as Pascal said, "The heart has its reasons that reason does not know."

We hope in this book to get to the heart of friendship.

MURIEL JAMES
Lafayette, California

LOUIS M. SAVARY
South Belmar, New Jersey

The Heart of Friendship

❧ 1 ❧

Friends and Friendship

One's friends are that part of the human race
with which one can be human.

SANTAYANA

Friends

Everyone wants friends. Everyone needs good friends. Most people would like to have them.

For Cicero, friendship's worth was incalculable. "What sweetness is left in life, if you take away friendship?" he wrote. "Robbing life of friendship is like robbing the world of the sun."

Just about every philosopher, from Aristotle to Martin Buber, has tried to put into words the unique experience of being friends.

Leslie Weatherhead, theologian, tells a story of two friends during the war. When one was injured and could not get back to the trenches, the other went out to get him against his officer's orders. He returned mortally wounded and his friend, whom he had carried back, was dead.

The officer said, "It was not worth it."

The dying man replied, "But it was worth it, sir, because when I got to him he said, 'Jim, I knew you'd come.'"[1]

1. Leslie Weatherhead, *Prescription for Anxiety* (Nashville: Abingdon Press, 1956).

Theodore Rubin, psychiatrist, wrote of David and Lisa, two emotionally disturbed young people who lived in a mental institution. Both were out of contact; neither trusted people.

David had blocked off any feelings of closeness to others. He concentrated on mathematics, chess and mechanical drawing, and strongly refused any kind of physical touch.

Lisa avoided contact with people. She conversed but spoke only in rhymes.

Then, in a moment of bravery, David established contact with Lisa.

"Lisa, stay." He spoke very slowly and carefully.

Now he hesitated—then said, "Lisa, trust me."

She looked into his eyes. . . .

"Lisa." He swallowed hard. "Lisa, take my hand." [2]

For the first time, David chose to touch another person, and Lisa answered without rhyming.

The budding relationship between David and Lisa began to help their emotional health. Friendship gave them new life.

Friendship relationships often have a unique effect on the people involved, sometimes making them feel loved and cared for, sometimes giving their life meaning and purpose, sometimes uncovering their hidden strengths. People shape their friendships; their friendships shape them.

In his famous book, *The City of God*, completed in 427 A.D., Augustine said that friendship was higher than any other form of human love; he prayed for it and put all his efforts into developing it. Even as an old man of seventy, he spoke of friendship as his one true consolation.

From birth to death, friendship adds meaning and sparkle to all of life. Yet, for various reasons, many people have never experienced it.

2. Theodore Isaac Rubin, *Lisa and David* (New York: Ballantine Books, 1962), p. 105.

❦ *"People shape their friendships,*
their friendships shape them"

The German poets Goethe and Schiller were slow to discover it. For seven years they lived as mutually indifferent neighbors. Each knew the other's work but neither made an effort toward friendship. In 1794, they met casually at a scientific lecture, agreed to visit, and soon became close friends.[3]

This importance of friendship is reflected in Goethe's poem:

> The world is so empty
> if one thinks only
> of mountains, rivers, and
> cities; but to know someone
> who thinks and feels with me,
> and who, though distant
> is close to me in spirit,
> this makes the earth for me
> an inhabited garden.

How to find friends and keep them? How to love them and grow with them? How to be friends in spite of differences in values and personalities and without limiting the other person's freedom. That's the challenge.

Vance Packard quoted a wife who faced the challenge of friendship when her husband was considering relocating for a better job:

> I think sooner or later every family has to decide what is more important—money and position or roots. For me, family and friends—*old* friends—mean a great deal. . . . I think the security of having a real home with family and friends around that I don't have to say goodby to again means more to me than the security of a bigger pay check.[4]

Friends are important. Whether new or old they are a powerful force in life. However, because the power of friendship is often hidden, it is largely unexplored. Because this power is unexplored, it goes untapped.

3. Calvin Thomas, "Schiller," *Encyclopedia Americana* (1953), XXIV: 372.
4. Vance Packard, *A Nation of Strangers* (New York: David McKay, 1972), p. 146.

A Low Priority

Social sciences emphasize certain human relationships—marriage, family, political groups, street gangs, corporate structures, and others. In striking contrast friendship has received relatively little serious study by psychologists, sociologists, anthropologists, and the like.[5]

While much research is done on relationships such as teacher-student, parent-child, therapist-client, employer-employee, and so on, the many varieties of friendship are usually lumped together with other kinds of relationships in a vague category called "interpersonal relations." As a result, friendship remains one of the least explored and researched areas of human relationship.

Yet, in spite of the low priority assigned to its study, many social scientists, including the authors of this book, admit strong personal concern about friendship in their own lives.

What "Friend" Means

According to poet Ralph Waldo Emerson, "a friend is a person with whom I may be sincere." That's somewhat different from Webster's dictionary, which defines a friend as: "One attached to another by esteem, respect and affection; an intimate."

Although the dictionary defines the *word* "friend," it does not describe the *experience* of being a friend. Read the dictionary definition again, then recall times when you felt healed or affirmed by being with a special friend, or times when you felt empty because of a friend's absence. The experience of any word is often deeper than its definition, so Webster's words do not begin to suggest the commitment many friends feel toward each other.

---

5. *International Encyclopedia of the Social Sciences*, David L. Sills, ed., Vol. 6 (New York: Macmillan, 1968), pp. 12–17.

However, friend, as a word, is frequently used in ways that imply definitions. Comments such as the following are not uncommon:

> "Well, if she's such a good friend, why can't she spend more time with you than with her husband?"

> "I know that he has other obligations, but he's my friend, and why is he always busy just when I need him the most?"

> "I used to think he was my friend, but now he's not interested in anything except work."

> "Why can't we just be friends, instead of lovers?"

> "My friend got killed, and I'll never get over it."

> "My family isn't half as important to me as my buddies. Friends are the people I can really count on."

> "Sometimes when I'm near my best friend, I get a little scared and feel as if I need to crack a joke or turn on the TV, or do something to break the intensity of it all."

> "I'd give a lot to have a good friend, the kind I really need, but I'm so busy I don't have the time to do anything about it."

People use emotion-laden expressions like these to describe feelings and experiences connected with friends, but the meaning of "friend" remains unclear. Adjectives often used to describe them are vague and primitive ones like, "good," "close," "casual," "special," or "very best."

Sometimes the word "friend" itself is more confusing than clarifying, because people use the same term to describe members of a bowling team, beer-drinking buddies, a man and his dog, or husbands and wives. In fact, some people use the label *friend* for anyone not their enemy.

Images of Friendship

To help understand friendship and its potentials, new descriptions of friendship are needed.

In a recent workshop, some people used comparisons to describe friendship in new ways and found that each one brought out a different insight.

> "Friendship is like a diamond in the rough that needs to be cut with loving care so that all its facets are brought to their clearest potential."

> "Friendship is like a surprise birthday present tied with bright paper and ribbons. The excitement is in discovering what's inside."

> "Friendship is like the first spring day after a dismal winter. It warms the heart with beauty."

> "Friendship is like a high flying kite that responds to the string held gently in the hand of the flyer."

> "Friendship is like the sand and the sea where the tide ebbs and falls in ever-changing, ever-predictable dances."

Comparisons expand the mind like kaleidoscopes that offer new designs every time you twist them—each image used to describe friendship offers new ways of thinking about it.

Imaginary Friends

Out of the need for friendship, many children create imaginary friends who seem as real to them as living persons.

According to Robert Louis Stevenson, friends, imaginary or real, can be called "a present you give yourself." His poem "The Unseen Playmate" describes one child's imaginary friend:

> He lies in the laurels, he runs on the grass,
> He sings when you tinkle the musical glass . . .
> He loves to be little, he hates to be big,
> 'Tis he that inhabits the caves that you dig . . .

Imaginary friendships have a strong effect on the people who create them. Sometimes imaginary friends play the role of listener when there is no sympathetic human ear nearby. They may build confidence on a scary journey or help pass the time in a lonely sick bed. They may take the blame for things that go wrong so that children may maintain a sense of their own self-esteem in a world where they always seem to be wrong or "in the way." [6]

Grownups have imaginary friends, too. They need not always be "human," but may be animals, spirits, or objects.

Harvey, the six-foot rabbit, who was companion, confidant and counselor of the grown man who created him, is one of the best-known imaginary friends.

Mountain climber Hermann Buhl was the first man to reach the summit of the Himalayas. He did the last stages of the climb alone—but not really alone. During hours of extreme tension and loneliness, he claims to have had a "partner" with him, an imaginary friend who looked after him, took care of him, strengthened him.[7]

Many adults have imaginary friends like Buhl's to comfort and guide them, talk over problems and suggest solutions to predicaments. Some refer to their imaginary friends as inner voices they hear or simply describe the experience as "talking to myself."

Both adults and children in order to concretize their imaginary friends, will talk to a teddy bear, hug a blanket or write in a diary. Anne Frank described her diary as a friend, and even named it "Kitty."

Christopher Robin in A. A. Milne's classic, *Winnie the Pooh*, created a whole world of imaginary animal friends like Pooh Bear, Piglet and Eeyore the Donkey.

Some people look forward to spending a few moments each day with imaginary friends like Charlie Brown and Snoopy in the newspaper comic strips. In 1916, long before *Peanuts* began to appear, newspaper readers shared the friendships between Archy, a philosophical cockroach who used a type-

6. Selma H. Fraiberg, *The Magic Years: Understanding and Handling the Problems of Early Childhood* (New York: Charles Scribner's Sons, 1959), pp. 141–145.
7. Hermann Buhl, *Lonely Challenge*, trans. Hugh Merrik (New York, E. P. Dutton, 1956), p. 292.

writer to communicate, and Mehitabel, an amorous, worldly wise cat. Besides telling about their escapades, Archy's mission in life was

> to bring humans and cockroaches into a better understanding with each other, to establish some sort of hands across the kitchen sink arrangement.[8]

Archy was perhaps the one cockroach in history that people liked as a friend.

A Universe of Friendship

The philosopher George Santayana's definition of friends as "that part of the human race with which one can be human" may seem too limiting to some people.

They report friendships with *real* animals, plants, trees, as well as with imaginary people, animals, and things. They may claim that "a man's best friend is his dog," or more humorously that "diamonds are a girl's best friend."

The experiences such people have sometimes have an eerie quality. On June 22, 1974, the *San Francisco Chronicle* related a strange incident. Here is the story exactly as the newspaper reported it:

> A giant sea turtle saved the life of a 52-year-old woman lost at sea for two days after a shipwreck in the Philippines.
>
> The Manila newspaper, *Bulletin Today*, identified the woman as Candelaria Villanueva, a passenger on the Philippine inter-island vessel, *Aloha*, which burned and sank off Zamboanga Del Norte province June 2. Four of the vessel's 271 passengers died.
>
> Mrs. Villanueva had been adrift for 48 hours when she was sighted by a Navy ship riding on the back of the giant turtle. She looked haggard and hysterical.
>
> Navy Lieutenant Cesario Mana was quoted by the newspaper:

---

8. Don Marquis, *The Life and Times of Archy and Mehitabel* (New York: Collier, 1925), p. 17.

"I would not have believed it if I had merely heard about it. But I was an eyewitness myself, along with my shipmates."

After the woman was pulled up onto the ship, the turtle "even circled the area twice before disappearing into the sea, as if to reassure itself that its former passenger was in good hands," said the officer.

Agence France-Pressee

Would you call the relationship between the sea turtle and the woman friendship or not?

John Lilly, psychiatrist and researcher who studied the behavior of dolphins for years in Florida, claims that in many ways dolphins are smarter than humans and capable of friendship.[9] He describes how they are able to trust and play with persons they know.

Lions are also capable of friendship says Joy Adamson in *Born Free.*

Martin Buber, philosopher, revealed his transcendent feelings of friendship with his horse. He was eleven years old, spending the summer on his grandparents' estate. Often he would steal unobserved into the stable to make contact with a broad dapple-gray horse. It was not a casual delight to him, nor was it just a friendly encounter. It was a deeply stirring happening. Buber remembered it many years later:

> I must say that what I experienced in touch with the animal was the Other, the immense otherness of the Other. . . . it let me approach, confided itself to me, placed itself elementally in the relation of *Thou* and *Thou* with me.[10]

Jane van Lawick-Goodall, known for her work with wild chimpanzees, had a similar mystical experience:

> I was alone with David, a chimp, that day, deep in the forest. I held out a palm nut to him and, although he did not want it, he accepted my offering. For a full ten seconds, he held my

9. John Lilly, *Man and Dolphin* (New York: Pyramid Publications, 1961), pp. 104–105, 121–129.
10. Martin Buber, *Between Man and Man* (New York: Macmillan, 1965), pp. 22–23.

hand gently and firmly in his. Finally, with a last glance at the nut, he let it fall to the ground.

> In that brief exalted moment, I felt a thrill of communication with a wild chimpanzee. . . . He had reached out to reassure me by the pressure of his fingers. Although he rejected my gift, he gave me one of his own: a primitive communion based on touch, so distinct from the sophisticated communion based in intellect.[11]

Plants may also become friends. Psychiatrist Viktor Frankl tells of a lonely young woman in a concentration camp who developed a friendship with a tree:

> Pointing through the window of the hut, she said, "This tree here is the only friend I have in my loneliness." Through that window she could see just one branch of a chestnut tree, and on the branch were two blossoms. "I often talk to this tree," she said to me. I was startled and didn't quite know how to take her words. Was she delirious? Did she have occasional hallucinations? Anxiously, I asked her if the tree replied. "Yes." What did it say to her? She answered, "It said to me, 'I'm here—I am here—I am life, eternal life.'"[12]

Because of these kinds of friendships that people experience, perhaps Santayana's definition could be expanded to read, "One's friends are those parts of the *universe* with which one can be truly human."

Some might argue against the possibility of being friends with the universe. Not humanistic ecologists. They could claim that whereas animals and plants are obviously capable of responding to people, the universe includes many seemingly inanimate objects such as rocks and stars, which might also respond in some form of friendship. Some people do form unusual friendships with just such things. In Mexico, people can buy alabaster rocks which are shaped like eggs. They are

11. Jane van Lawick-Goodall, *My Friends: The Wild Chimpanzees* (Washington, D.C.: National Geographic Society, 1967), pp. 191–192.
12. Viktor Frankl, *Man's Search for Meaning: An Introduction to Logotherapy* (New York: Simon & Schuster, 1969), pp. 109–110.

꧁ "One's friends are those parts of the universe
with which one can be truly human"

meant to be held, touched, rubbed, and carried as constant companions.

One old woman collected rocks from all over the world. She kept them in her room and talked to them as old friends.

She picked up a speckled pebble from her dresser and smiled at it. "It's brimming with memories. Each stone in my room hides generations of experience within it. Each one holds special meanings for me."

When asked if she preferred her rock friends above human friends, "No," she said, "but rocks are more trustworthy than some people. Besides, my rock friends are always faithfully here."

Other people feel an affinity to other parts of the universe. The Bushmen of Africa feel a friendship with the stars. They claim the stars talk to them, laugh with them, and guide them.[13]

Antoine de Saint-Exupery's Little Prince also locates friendship among the stars and tells his friend that after he dies he will become a star.

> You will love to watch all the stars in the heavens. . . . They will all be your friends. . . . You—you alone—will have the stars as no one else has them. . . .
>
> In one of the stars I shall be living. In one of them I shall be laughing. And so it will be as if all the stars were laughing, when you look at the sky at night. . . .
>
> You—only you—will have stars that can laugh! [14]

Friendships, like stars, can never be replaced.

Each friendship, like each star, has a life of its own! No two friendships are identical. People who are fortunate enough to have several, discover they are all different.

Therefore, each can be celebrated.

13. Laurens van der Post, *The Lost World of the Kalahari* (New York: Wm. Morrow, 1958).

14. Antoine de Saint-Exupery, *The Little Prince* (New York: Harcourt, Brace & Co., 1943), p. 85.

ᴥ૬ 2 ૬ᴥ

The Third Self of Friendship

> The meeting of two personalities is like the contact of two chemical substances; if there is any reaction, both are transformed.
>
> CARL JUNG

The Special Feeling

Friendship is a special kind of human experience.

One person might explain the special feeling by saying, "We understand each other because we're on the same wave length."

Another might say, "We are free to be ourselves with each other and don't have to worry about what people say."

A third: "Our friendship is like a protective cloud that surrounds us, and when we're together we feel safe, secure and trusting."

Or: "Whenever I'm with friends I'm open to new ideas and experiences and that is exciting."

The secret of that fresh, alive, open and excited feeling seems to be that friendship provides a chance to live a new life. "Friendship is a second existence," explained Baltasar Gracian.

People talk about friendship as if it had a life of its own: being born, growing, passing through crises, weakening and sometimes dying.

Perhaps this way of talking about friendship provides the most fundamental insight of all—that *friendship is a thing in itself*, that is real, unique and personal. It can be called a *third self*, a new reality distinct from the friends themselves.

Mathematics of Friendship

People tend to describe friendship from at least three different perspectives. Each may be summarized in a sort of "friendship mathematics."

Viewpoint 1. According to this view, friendship is so important that people are incomplete (only half persons) unless they have their other halves. Or, mathematically:

$$½ \text{ person} + ½ \text{ person} \rightarrow 1 \text{ person}$$

Viewpoint 2. Friendship seen this way is not the sum of the individuals involved, as in viewpoint 1; it is not meant to melt people together but to develop their unique differences. Mathematically Viewpoint 2 is stated as follows:

$$1 \text{ person} + 1 \text{ person} \rightarrow 1 \text{ person} + 1 \text{ person}$$

From this viewpoint, friendship enhances and enriches each person but in the end there are still two people relating freely and independently.

Viewpoint 3. The third-self theory suggests that a friendship has a life of its own and a radically new mathematics:

$$1 \text{ person} + 1 \text{ person} \rightarrow 1 \text{ person} + 1 \text{ person} + 1 \text{ third self}$$

Not only do friends maintain their individual identities and become enriched in the process, but a new personal reality may be experienced.

This reality, friendship's third self, may be described as a *meta-person* or a *meta-self*, since it is more than an ordinary person and beyond a single self. *Meta* is a Greek prefix meaning "beyond," "transcending" or "higher."

Viewpoint 1

Romeo and Juliet is a classic example of this first viewpoint which is still very common today. In a song made famous by singer Barbra Streisand about "people who need people," the lyrics contain a line, "You were half, now you're whole," expressing Viewpoint 1.

Viewpoint 1 sees individuals in a deep friendship losing their original identities, as hydrogen and oxygen, in combining to form water, lose their original identities.

Some people who experience a lover's friendship in this way speak of being "made for each other." For them, friendship feels so ecstatic, so deep and integral, so natural and right, that it seems to uncover a personal bond made ages ago, as if the relationship had been waiting for eternity to be realized in this moment.

Surrealist André Breton, speaking to his friend, began, "Before I knew you . . . ," Then he caught himself and said,

> Before I knew you—look, the words are meaningless. You know very well that, *when I saw you for the first time, I recognized you at once.*

This first view of friendship has deep historical roots in both Eastern and Western civilizations.

The Upanishads, ancient sacred writings of the East, explained how each person alone remained incomplete, and became whole only in a heterosexual relationship:

> Each man is only half. The empty space is filled by the woman. He coupled with her. So it is that people were created.

According to the Bible, the original woman was formed from Adam's rib. Only together did they become complete. Eve was "half" of him—some would say "the better half."

Western civilization also stressed this half-plus-half idea in relationships between men and men, between women and women. Ancient classical authors contrasted the incompleteness of friendless people with the wholeness of friendship. The Greek philosopher Plato described a man with a friend as a *whole man.* For Aristotle, friendship was as "a single soul dwelling in two bodies." Among ancient Greek men, friendship meant a man-man relationship, often homosexual. This was also true of some Greek women.

In the seventh century B.C., on the Greek island of Lesbos lived a poetess named Sappho, whose fame rivaled Homer's. Head of a girl's school, she encouraged woman-woman friendships and said that her woman friend, Atthis, could make her "heart to flame up and burn with love." When Atthis was leaving, Sappho wrote,

> I shall never see Atthis again and
> I surely wish I were dead.

Centuries later, this first viewpoint of friendship continued to prevail. Both Cicero and St. Jerome referred to friends as "a part of my soul." To St. Ambrose, a friend was the "better portion" and the "larger part" of himself. In medieval monasteries, people frequently spoke of a friend as "*half* of my soul." [1]

If these classical writers are interpreted literally, a friendless person is less than human, not fully a self. For them, to be without a friend would mean to be without integral identity. However, in such a half-plus-half viewpoint, it seems that a person could have only one true friend at a time. Since many people enjoy more than one friendship, a question comes to mind: How many "halves" does a person have available for friendship?

Viewpoint 2

Viewpoint 2 would assert that individuality is not lost in friendship but is enriched. It says, "A friendship is nothing more than a you-plus-me" or "It's the sum of two individuals"

1. For a survey of friendship from ancient times through the twelfth century, see Adele M. Fiske, R.S.C.J., *The Survival and Development of the Ancient Concept of Friendship in the Early Middle Ages*, unpublished doctoral thesis, Fordham University, New York.

or "A friendship has no life of its own different from my life or your life."

That Viewpoint 2 is in clear contrast with Viewpoint 1 is seen in the ways people view marriage relationships.

Viewpoint 1 couples describe their marriages in *symbiotic* terms: together the partners enjoy a single shared life.

"My wife and I are one body and one mind," explained a husband. "Together we are one. Without each other we would be incomplete."

Viewpoint 2 married couples stress their own individuality. Though committed to the relationship, they assert, "I am myself and you are yourself." One spouse expressed Viewpoint 2 this way:

> I want to do my thing and you want to do your thing. At the same time, I want you to become your maximum self and expect you to allow me to become my maximum self, too. This is the essential meaning of our relationship.

Viewpoint 2 relationships tend to grow deeper as friends become more fully themselves. Sharing is at its highest, paradoxically, when "distance" between relating partners is greatest. Exchange of ideas, feelings and secrets at the deepest level is possible because the friend is felt most intensely as *another* person.

Viewpoint 2 friendship was succinctly summed up by Gestalt psychologist Fritz Perls:

> I do my thing, and you do your thing. I am not in this world to live up to your expectations, and you are not in this world to live up to mine. You are you, and I am I: if by chance we find each other, it's beautiful. If not, it can't be helped.[2]

Only recently has the second viewpoint on friendship come into prominence, but to many people it opens friendship to a richness and freedom that Viewpoint 1 fails to offer.

2. Frederick Perls, *Gestalt Therapy Verbatim* (Lafayette, Calif.: Real People Press, 1969), p. 4.

Various human liberation movements encourage Viewpoint 2 relationships between men and men, women and women, and men and women. Stressing equality, their mottoes underline the fact that each person has special talents and unique gifts to develop and that these potentials go unrealized because people traditionally relate to each other in inequality-laden ways.

According to Viewpoint 2, friends work well together when each maintains distinctness and separation from the other. Pairs of comedians often owe their onstage effectiveness to strong personality differences. The biting and satirical Bob Hope worked well with the relaxed Bing Crosby. Fat and fidgety Oliver Hardy blended with Stan Laurel, who was skinny and deadpanned. Sophisticated Johnny Carson needed good-time Ed McMahon to be the butt of his jokes and teasing. Pairs of musical collaborators with very different personalities—Gilbert and Sullivan, Rodgers and Hart, Lerner and Loewe—combined to produce shows that rank high in the world of musical comedy.

Huntley and Brinkley, the famous newscast team, first came together to cover the political conventions in October 1956. When an interviewer asked if they had any specific reactions to each other *just as people*, not necessarily as professional announcers, they replied:

> *Huntley:* The realization came very fast that here was a decent guy, very easy to work with and a pro.

> *Brinkley:* I never even thought about it, and I think the fact that nothing struck me is probably the reason it worked. *We just sort of took each other as we were, and we still do.* Personality has never been a problem. It isn't because either of us is so nice, or smart, or anything like that. For one thing, neither of us is an exhibitionist. Neither of us has any interest in hogging the air. I don't care who gets on the air, really I don't. Neither of us is trying to prove anything or win anything.[3]

3. James F. Fixx, "An Anniversary Talk With Huntley & Brinkley," *McCall's*, October 1966, pp. 59, 176.

The essential characteristic of Viewpoint 2 is that each friend accepts the other as unique and different. Friendship is viewed as something to help preserve and enhance this uniqueness and difference.

Viewpoint 3

Without contradicting the second viewpoint, third-self people suggest that a friendship relationship offers something more. To prove their point, they might propose the following simple experiment.

On a piano, play two or three different notes, one at a time. Notice that each individual sound is very special and unique. Then play the same notes all at the same time and listen. Together, the notes form *a new kind of sound*, unlike any of the notes played separately.

When two or three piano notes are struck simultaneously, a musical relationship is created which musicians describe as a chord. In a similar way, Viewpoint 3 people feel that a close friendship, without destroying individual identities, creates a new kind of self. I can go to a party without you and, like a single piano note, express myself as a "me." You can go without me and, like a different single note, express yourself as a "you." But if we go to the party together then, we might express ourselves as a "we." A third self of friendship is acting when friends experience things together, like piano notes played together to create a new kind of sound, and if all the people at the party are friends, their "group third-self" might sound like an orchestra.

A third self of friendship happens when two people, like two notes, come together in such a way that, without losing their individualities, they form a new entity.

This third self of friendship is a new creation, a meta-self. And, like a kiss, it takes two people relating to make it happen.

The Realm of "Between"

According to Jewish philosopher Martin Buber, friendship occurs in the "realm of 'between.'" For him, "between" is a new

"A 'group third-self' might sound like an orchestra"

reality and it is an alternative to isolated individualism or to losing oneself in collective relationships. Like a third self, it cannot be seen, only experienced.

> On the far side of the subjective,
> on this side of the objective,
> on the narrow ridge,
> where I and Thou meet,
> there is the realm of "between."
>
> This reality, whose disclosure
> has begun in our time,
> shows the way,
> leading beyond individualism
> and collectivism,
> for the life decision
> of future generations.[4]

Unfortunately, some people may never discover the land of "between," or adventure far enough to form a third self. But when a third self is created, such a friendship involves three selves—you, me, and our relationship.

Sometimes friendship's third self shows itself to be clearly different from each of the friends. For example, two individuals may act one way when alone, but very differently when together as friends in the realm of between.

This is the experience of two accountants. At their desks they are usually very quiet and intent on their work; but when they get together as friends at the water cooler, they often explode with jokes and laughter.

Friendship makes people different.

For Buber, the future of humanity depends upon a rebirth of dialogue, or, in other words, exploring "the between" mode of experience. In its fullest blossoming, this could lead people to third-self friendships with all the universe—the sea turtles and trees, the rocks and the stars—as well as with each other.[5]

---

4. Martin Buber, *Between Man and Man* (London: Collins, 1947), p. 204. Sense-lining added.
5. See Martin Buber, *Between Man and Man* (New York: Macmillan, 1948), pp. 204 ff.

"In friendship there are no gifted or ungifted, only those who give themselves and those who withhold themselves"

Spheres of Dialogue

For Buber, there are four spheres of dialogue. Each of them needs to be rediscovered among humans today.

Each forms an element of possible cosmic friendship.

The *first sphere* involves relating to the inanimate world, everything "from stones to stars."

Ecologists assert the organic unity of the whole universe, with human life as an integral part of this unity. People are inextricably intertwined with all the elements—soil, air, water, minerals. All these enter a person's personal sphere. The inanimate world permits itself to be experienced by people.[6]

The interdependence between humans and the world is so complete, wrote ecologist René Dubos, that "in practice, we do not live *on* the planet earth but *with* the life it harbors and *within* the environment that life creates." [7]

The *second sphere* involves dialogue with living things such as plants and animals. Here, people invite animals or plants into their personal human sphere. They allow creatures to respond from the whole of their being, to the fullest extent of dialogue.[8]

"I said to the almond tree, 'Friend, speak to me of God,' and the almond tree blossomed," said Nicolas Kazantazakis.

Reverence in the face of nature survives today in people's awareness of their kinship to all other living things.

But reverence is not enough, Buber and others would argue, because people have never been passive witnesses of nature.

6. See Martin Buber, *I and Thou* (New York: Charles Scribner's Sons, 1958), p. 5.

7. René Dubos, *A God Within* (New York: Charles Scribner's Sons, 1972), p. 34.

8. See Martin Buber, *I and Thou* (New York: Charles Scribner's Sons, 1958), pp. 6 ff. Cf. Muriel James, *Born to Love, Transactional Analysis in the Church* (Reading, Mass.: Addison-Wesley, 1973), pp. 187–197.

By their very presence, people change the environment. The challenge is to see humanity and nature as complementary components, each shaping the other in a continuous act of creation. In the words of René Dubos,

> To be creative, man must relate to nature with his senses as much as with his common sense, with his heart as much as with his knowledge. He must read the book of external nature and the book of his own nature, to discern the common patterns and harmonies.[9]

The *third sphere* of relating is that of "spirit." It asks humans to enter into dialogue with books and writings, with all works of art, science, or handicraft that reveal the "spirits" of their makers. The writer's words, the piece of sculpture, the potter's vase, each confronts people and demands response from them.[10]

A woman entered the Fifth Avenue Bookshop and asked for help.

> You see, a friend wrote me a letter and told me about the book. I've lost the letter, and I can't remember the name of the book or of the author. But there was something my friend quoted from the book. It said, "Your pain is the breaking of the shell that encloses your understanding."

The woman repeated the line as though it had penetrated her and released some deep feelings.

The bookseller went to the shelf and took down a copy of Kahlil Gibran's *The Prophet* and turned to the chapter on pain. She showed it to the woman.

> I remember the look that swept across her sweet little old face. She took the book into her hand. She read the line, the page. She went and sat down. . . . And she read, entirely oblivious of me and of everything but what was before her on the page.[11]

9. René Dubos, *A God Within* (New York: Charles Scribner's Sons, 1972), p. 173.
10. See Martin Buber, *I and Thou* (New York: Charles Scribner's Sons, 1958), p. 101.
11. Barbara Young, *This Man from Lebanon: A Study of Kahlil Gibran* (New York: Knopf, 1945), pp. 14–16.

The woman had entered the third sphere of relating. She was in touch with the spirit of Kahlil Gibran.

The *fourth sphere* involves dialogue between two or more people in which each person experiences mutual affirmation and acceptance. In this fourth sphere a sense of we-ness develops between people that can lead to a third self friendship.[12]

Ultimately, the fourth sphere could lead to universal friendship embracing all races and nations.

In a meeting on world government, it was said:

> When we talk of transcending nationalism, it cannot be to achieve planetary uniformity. It is something much more complex, human, and loveable. It must be based on forms of cooperation which respect local autonomy, which respect diversity, yet build the essential unities of our new global society.[13]

This is not an intellectual activity, according to Buber. "There are no gifted nor ungifted here, only those who give themselves and those who withhold themselves." [14]

When humans develop and are integrating all four spheres of dialogue, the world will be ready for universal friendship. Until then, close and third-self friendships must suffice. This book focuses primarily on friendships between people. It also points to the future and to the possibility of something more.

Friendship's third self is impossible to create without the essential parts—two or more friends who are willing to enter the world of the between. When together, they *may* evolve a new reality which is distinguishable from each of them.

Building a third self of friendship is easier if the friends in-

12. See Martin Buber, *I and Thou* (New York: Charles Scribner's Sons, 1958), p. 102.

13. Quoted in Maurice E. Strong, ed., *Who Speaks for Earth?* (New York: W. W. Norton, 1973), p. 26.

14. Martin Buber, *Between Man and Man* (Boston: Beacon Press, 1955), p. 35.

volved realize they are indeed creating something new and that it is one of the most important things people can do in life.

A thousand years ago, a wise Hindu Bhartrihari asked, "If a man has a friend, what need has he of medicines?"

Members of a Meta-Self

This meta-self may be compared to a *corporation*. When a group of people create a business relationship among themselves, their corporate relationship is recognized legally as a "person." Whether a giant like IBM or General Motors, or as small as Bill 'n' Sally's Diner, Inc., each corporation is treated by law *as a new person*.

Viewpoint 3 suggests that each close friendship be treated *as a new person*.

In many ways, corporations act like persons. They pay taxes, make decisions, spend money, go to court, try to influence people, and relate to other corporations. In its own way, a friendship can act as a unit toward other people.

A corporation, like a friendship, may operate distinctly from the individual selves involved in it. It may be interested in buying oil wells, while some of its members (living their own lives) may choose to invest in real estate. Or, while some individual members may die, the corporation lives on. New individuals may join the corporation, or the members may choose to dissolve it. In other words, a corporation, like a friendship, may operate as a meta-person with a life different from the lives of each of its members.

Naming a Third Self

Some friends give a new name to their third self, in much the same way that a group of people identify their relationship by a corporate name.

Physician Michael Samuels and friend Hal Bennett gave their third self the name *Kishah*.

In their introduction to *Spirit Guides*, they explained how their book was written by one person, despite the fact that there were two authors. Their method of writing was to sit down together, relax, then focus on a particular set of ideas. Although the two friends spoke back and forth as they wrote,

> . . . the experience is like two voices in one consciousness.
> . . . The two authors feel that their voices merge *to create a third voice that has an identity all its own.* . . .

They realized that this third voice was itself a *spirit guide*. And so they decided to give this guide full credit as the author of the book and to look upon themselves as *channels* through whom the guide would speak.

The name of their spirit guide author is *Kishah*. The name means "mountain of energy." It is pronounced "Kee-sha." [15]

Just as corporations develop their own identities, families may develop their own "group self." People sometimes treat families as entities when they describe them as a whole: "That creative Smith family" or "The Browns are always punctual people" or "Here come the fun-loving Hendersons."

Group names are not a modern development. American Indian tribes had clearly identifiable names. Totem poles describing them stood prominently in their villages. African groups often named themselves after animals whose qualities they desired to emulate. American sports teams even carry group names such as Redskins, Jets, Dolphins, Colts, and Angels. Team members wear identical symbols on their uniforms.

Sociologists who study groups of people never tire of reminding their students that "groups are real." Whether it be the Kelly family, the Flatbush Avenue Gang, the local P.T.A., the Black Panthers, or the United States Navy, each group has its own identity, personality, characteristics and needs.

A group is or can become a new self, a meta-self. On a football

---

15. Michael Samuels, M.D. and Hal Bennett, *Spirit Guides: Access to Inner Worlds* (New York: Random House, 1974), p. 1. Italics added.

team, for example, players may have third selves with other players, and the team *as a whole* may also experience a group third self.

Identifying Views of Friendship

Usually, an outside observer cannot tell if friends view their relationship as Viewpoint 1, 2, or 3.

Some friendships seem to defy classification. For example, Kahlil Gibran, author of *The Prophet*, enjoyed a close friendship with his companion-secretary Barbara Young. For most of the last seven years of his life, she lived with Gibran and his wife.

To Barbara Young, Gibran was "a close and beloved friend." To Gibran, the relationship was named "poets working together in Beauty's name."

From time to time, to symbolize their friendship, Gibran would suggest that the two of them eat their soup from one bowl. Barbara described the scene.

> We would arrange the small table with one large bowl of soup. There were always croutons, many croutons, and the soup was thick, a puree. We would be seated with ceremony. Then, taking the soup spoon, Gibran would draw an imaginary line through the middle of the soup, saying with the greatest gravity, "This is your half of the soup, and your half of the croutons, and this other is my half. See to it that we neither one trespass upon the soup and the croutons of the other!" [16]

Then they would laugh. For they knew it was as impossible to separate the lives of friends as to draw a line through a bowl of soup.

Gibran's friendship with Barbara Young, as well as his symbolic soup ceremony, seems open to interpretation by advocates of all three viewpoints on friendship. Viewpoint 1 would

16. Barbara Young, *This Man from Lebanon: A Study of Kahlil Gibran*, p. 29.

emphasize the single bowl of soup: "The two portions of soup, like the two friends, were totally intermingled." Viewpoint 2 might emphasize the essential freedom and independence of the two friends: "See to it that we neither one trespass upon the soup and croutons of the other." Viewpoint 3 points to three "selves" in the story: Gibran, Barbara and the third self symbolized by the bowl of soup. In most cases, only the friends themselves really know how they view their own friendship.

Friends who write to each other often do so as an expression of their friendship. Among hundreds of famous letter-writing friends, the most outstanding are twelfth-century philosophers Heloise and Peter Abelard, poets Elizabeth Barrett and Robert Browning, and novelist Horace Walpole and educator Horace Mann, who during a forty-six-year friendship exchanged 848 letters.

But not all expressions come to us from famous writers. Struggling to describe a third self experience, a person no different from most of us wrote to another with a terminal illness:

> I have missed seeing you and my thoughts are very strong and positive. They are of hope and love for you and a very positive desire to see you fully recovered. They are of all the things that you have meant to me and the insights you have given me. I know I've told you before, but perhaps you wouldn't mind hearing again, that no one has ever been so persistent in calling me to account—why do I think what I do, why do I take my stand where I am. These questions you asked of me are still in my mind.

> I do miss the discussions of other levels of consciousness. My beliefs have been vastly broadened through my contact with you. I now feel there are no limits except what we impose on ourselves—and that there is much more to our "being" than our biological minds can ever understand.

Easily Overlooked

Each friendship possesses a life of its own. But because this "life" can't be touched, tasted, smelled, or seen the way cars and pianos can, it is easy to overlook.

A potential third self needs to be nourished and kept alive. Some friends worry about each other but overlook the relationship itself.

Two women had developed a third self of friendship, but recently one of the friends claimed, "Nowadays my friend calls only to discuss her own personal problems. I was worried about our friendship falling apart, so I told her, 'All you call me for is to moan and groan about yourself. You don't seem interested in *our relationship* anymore.' "

The third self of friendship seems to have been forgotten. If the women continue in this way, their third self's health is likely to suffer.

The same thing may happen in a family. Many responsible parents take care of their children's needs without ever relating to them as friends or forming third selves with their children.

Where there are no vital third selves, family members live apart from each other. At the dinner table they may be politely responsive when someone asks for pepper or potatoes, but seldom otherwise exchange their feelings and ideas, or do things together. In such families, parents and children often prefer to eat alone so that they can avoid each other.

When, in contrast, family members enjoy friendships with each other, a number of third selves will be happily interacting at the dinner table.[17] They will be sensitive to each other's joys as well as to each other's griefs.

Will Rogers, America's comic and ambassador of goodwill in the 1920s, developed this atmosphere in his own family.

17. For a discussion of ways to stimulate closer relationships among family members, see Muriel James *Transactional Analysis for Moms and Dads* (Reading, Mass.: Addison-Wesley, 1974).

Will Rogers once refused to "lay off" an old cowhand because Jimmy, the youngest child, liked the old man and spoke of him as a friend. That young friendship had a life of its own and Will Rogers was not about to destroy it.[18]

There is an ancient Zen story called "True Friends" that captures one experience of friendship:

> A long time ago in China there were two friends, one who played the harp skillfully and one who listened skillfully.
>
> When the one played or sang about a mountain, the other would say: "I can see the mountain before us."
>
> When the one played about water, the listener would exclaim: "Here is the running stream!"
>
> But the listener fell sick and died. The first friend cut the strings of his harp and never played again. Since that time the cutting of harp strings has always been a sign of intimate friendship.[19]

18. P. J. O'Brien, *Will Rogers: Ambassador of Good Will, Prince of Wit and Wisdom* (1935), p. 276.
19. Reported in Paul Reps, *Zen Flesh, Zen Bones* (Garden City, N.Y.: Doubleday), pp. 70–71.

❧ 3 ❧

The Process of Friendship

There is no shop anywhere where one can buy
friendship. . . .

The Little Prince
ANTOINE DE SAINT-EXUPERY

Choices in Friendship

Third-self friendship is exciting. Those who have it know
that it can't be bought, sold, or traded. It can only be entered into freely.

Some people are content with one deep friendship—raised to
the level of a third self. Like Henry Brooks Adams, they
say, "One friend in a lifetime is much, two are many; three
are hardly possible."

Or they may limit themselves to two or three third selves,
claiming, "I only have time for a very few close friends.
That's enough."

Still others seem able to sustain many friendships, most of them
"casual," only a few "close." Usually, only the closest friendships develop a meta-person—a third self. Perhaps there is
truth in the old proverb "A friend to everybody is a friend
to nobody."

In any case, choice is always involved. People can choose to
have casual, close or intimate friends. They can choose
whether or not to enter into a situation where a friendship

might be born. They can choose to give it life and growth. They can choose to let it die. Napoleon bragged that he never made friends, only courtiers. He died alone. The biblical story of Ruth tells of the friendship of two widows, Ruth and her mother-in-law, Naomi. To maintain her friendship with the older woman, Ruth chose to leave her homeland. She told Naomi,

> Don't ask me to go away from you, or to go back to my home. For where you go, I will go, and where you stay I shall stay. Your people shall be my people, and your God my God. Where you die, I will die, and there will I be buried (Ruth 2: 16–17).

The Process toward Friendship

The choices people make of whether or not to be friends and whether or not to become close friends seem to follow a certain process.

The process toward third-self friendship might be described in six general stages. The first stage is meeting in a matrix for friendship. Next in the process, people greet each other and get acquainted. They discover a sense of "we-ness." Out of this, a casual friendship begins to form. Building a close friendship is the next step and eventually, a third self of friendship may develop. This may be diagrammed in the following way:

matrix→acquaintanceship→"we"-ness→
casual friends→close friends→third self

A Matrix for Friendship

A *matrix for friendship* is simply a place or situation where things are happening and people can meet. It might be a bar, a factory, a club, a home, a school, a church or synagogue, a building, even a hospital, or a jail.

The matrix for Franklin Roosevelt and Eleanor was a Christmas party at the family home in Hyde Park. Anthropologists Margaret Mead and Ruth Benedict first met in a college classroom. Popular singers Carly Simon and James Taylor became

"Being in a matrix for friendship does not guarantee that friendship will occur"

friends during summers at the shore where their families vacationed.

Wherever there is more than one person, a matrix for friendship exists. An apartment with one person in it can be a matrix for reading, cooking, meditating or being creative. It is not, however, a matrix for friendship until other people are present.

A matrix for friendship is like a mixing bowl where ingredients for bread are mixed together. It is like a piano where keys wait to be played. It is like soil in which seeds may be planted.

Not all people within a matrix for friendship become acquainted. Being in a matrix for friendship does not guarantee that friendship will occur. Even though the matrix is there, the next step may not be taken.

Jamie Brown, a young man from St. Louis, went to college in hopes of making the friends he had never had. Though Jamie went to classes, mixers, plays, and sports events at school, he did not get to know anyone. He seldom made the effort to say Hello. Others seldom said Hello to him. Because he didn't reach out, he never formed personal bonds that could grow into friendship.

Getting Acquainted

What Do You Say after You Say Hello? is the provocative title of Eric Berne's last book. People know that what they say after they say Hello is very crucial, and friendliness is a basic ingredient for the next step. It means the difference between acceptance and rejection.

Some friends meet by accident and get acquainted by striking up a spontaneous conversation. New neighbors meet in the grocery store or across the backyard fence. Young people meet in school or at a dance, businessmen in an airplane or at a cocktail party.

Often friends become acquainted because a third person introduces them. Movie stars Spencer Tracy and Katharine Hepburn became acquainted through film director Joe Mankiewicz. As the story is told, Hepburn, though quite tall, wore specially built platform shoes in order to appear taller than men she met professionally. Describing the scene, a biographer wrote:

> Tracy was a big man—in every way—but not exceptionally tall: five feet ten and a half inches. When Joe Mankiewicz introduced them to each other, she looked Spencer over, tip to toe, as though she were considering buying him. Then she smiled her friendliest smile and said, "You're rather *short*, aren't you?"

> "Don't worry, honey," said Mankiewicz, trying desperately to extinguish Spencer's glare. "He'll cut you down to size." [1]

Frequently, people are afraid they won't have much to say after they say Hello. Such fears are usually groundless. As soon as they allow themselves to relax and be themselves, conversation begins to flow.

Years ago, when marriage partners were often selected by parents, and "courting" was a new-fangled idea, even prospective spouses used to wonder how they would become acquainted with each other. A scene from Thornton Wilder's play *Our Town* is a reminder of this.

> Dr. Gibbs: "Julia, do you know one of the things I was scared of when I married you?"

> Mrs. Gibbs: "Oh, go along with you!"

> Dr. Gibbs: "I was afraid we wouldn't have material for conversation more'n'd last us a few weeks." Both laugh. "I was afraid we'd run out and eat our meals in silence, that's a fact. —Well, you and I been conversing for twenty years now without any noticeable barren spells."

"Getting acquainted" is an important part of the friendship

---

1. Garson Kanin, *Tracy & Hepburn: An Intimate Memoir* (New York: Viking, 1971, Bantam Books ed.), pp. 3-4.

process, but greater satisfactions lie beyond the stage of acquaintanceship.

Discovering "We-ness"

People who share interests and do things together may begin to experience a "we-ness" with each other.

They will refer to themselves as "we," for example, "We're really enjoying ourselves," or "We both like horses," or "We plan to get together next week."

Harry S. Truman and his biographer, Merle Miller, became friends because they shared the childhood experience of wearing glasses.

"Well, sir," began Miller when first meeting Mr. Truman, "I've been wearing glasses since I was three years old, and I know you had to wear glasses as a boy. I wonder, sir, did they ever call you *four-eyes?*"

The President smiled and replied, "I've worn glasses since I was six years old, and, of course, they called me *four-eyes* and a lot of other things, too. That's hard on a boy. It makes him lonely, and it gives him an inferiority complex, and he has a hard time overcoming it." [2]

With these words began the relationship that eventually produced the best-selling book *Plain Speaking,* an oral biography of Truman.

The groups to which individuals belong and the people with whom they identify provide a sense of "we-ness." They may refer to themselves as "our family," "we stamp collectors," "we physicians," "our bridge club," "we who live in Scranton," "those of us who went to Harvard," or "the graduates of Lowell High School" and so on. Whether "we" situations happen between two people or among many, such inter-

2. Merle Miller, *Plain Speaking: An Oral Biography of Harry S. Truman* (New York: Berkley Publishing Co., 1974), p. 23.

personal situations are fertile ground for some level of friendship.

Casual Friendships

Bob Dylan met his high school sweetheart, Echo Helstrom, in an ice cream parlor. She was sitting with a girlfriend when Bob walked in with the boys in his band.

"We started talking about music," said Echo, "and Bob started talking to me about Howlin' Wolf and Jimmy Reed and B. B. King and all the great blues guys. I couldn't believe what he was saying. It couldn't be true . . . we could communicate on each other's level, speak the same language." [3]

People who see themselves having mutual interests, being together or doing something together frequently recognize a "we." Simply by talking together, they become aware of shared experiences, concerns, or interests.

A sense of casual friendship may be experienced between any two people, for example, husband and wife, study partners, tennis opponents, dancing partners, or couples on dates. It may also be experienced in larger groups such as families, school classes, sports teams, political parties, hobby clubs, professional organizations, religious groups, local communities, and citizens of a nation.

Many people choose not to develop deep friendships. Instead, they prefer casual relationships. This choice is often difficult for others to understand. At a recent party, Monica, a middle-aged widow with many close friends, struck up a conversation with a woman who had recently moved to town. The woman told Monica she would be moving again before the year was out, and that the company moved her husband to a new city about every three years. Monica was horrified.

The woman, in response, claimed, "Well, the kids won't like

3. Anthony Scaduto, *Bob Dylan: An Intimate Biography* (New York: Grosset and Dunlap, 1971), pp. 13–14.

it, and I'll hate the packing, but it's all part of being an executive's wife."

"But you must find it terrible to always be moving from your friends," argued Monica.

"One town is much like another," the woman responded. "I make new friends quickly and choose not to get overinvolved. It might upset me to leave."

Getting involved is, to some people, a negative situation. They choose to be neighborly, affable and friendly, keeping potential close friends at a distance.

Friendly people can be met at any bus station, bar or airport. They will disclose deep personal concerns in the first few minutes, but seldom reveal their names. They have no interest in close friendship or third-self friendship. If a relationship seems to be growing deep, they may drop it.

For these "friendly" people, friendship is not a "pearl of great price," but a useful commodity they can shop for along with the groceries. They might label a "friend" as anyone to whom they send a Christmas card with the message, "Let's get together soon."

Granted, the demanding pace of modern life greatly increases the fragility of relationships, making it difficult to start new friendships or preserve old ones. Frequent moves from one town, city or suburb to another can destroy the strands of friendship that are just beginning to weave themselves closely.

Unfortunately, friendship often becomes the pawn in a competitive, success-oriented society. Instead of nurturing deep friendships, some people use casual friends to "get ahead."

For business reasons, they may drop a friend's name, hoping that it will pay off, or maintain minimal contact, hoping that some day the friendship may prove "useful." They may call friends only when they need a favor.

Some people choose to have many casual friends and only a few close ones. They say it is impossible to spread their time, energy, and commitment too thin. They want to save themselves for those people who mean the most to them.

Close Friendships

As friendships deepen from casual to close, it becomes more and more difficult to draw the line between different stages. Often not even friends themselves can tell exactly when a friendship begins to be close. They may discover it long after it has happened.

In 1951, the home of crooner Nat King Cole was seized by the government because he was unable to pay $146,000 in back taxes. On a plane, two accountants, with offices in New York and Los Angeles, noticed Cole and his wife seated nearby. They had read of his tax problem. Phil Braunstein and his partner Harold Plant struck up a conversation with Cole and offered to help.

A few days later in Los Angeles, on the way to an after-meeting lunch, Nat made a gesture of friendship. "As they walked down the hall, still talking, Nat slipped his arm around Harold's shoulder," recalls Nat's wife, "a small, innocent, but warm gesture that Harold never forgot."

Many years later Harold explained, "It made me feel very odd and very proud, because I suddenly came to realize that Nat had not only accepted me as an accountant and business manager, but as a friend. It meant a great deal to me." [4]

Even after Nat's death, this friendship with Harold remained close with the entire Cole family.

Third-Self Friendship

A sense of "we-ness" may blossom quickly. But close friendships and a third self of friendship, which is a new being, may need much time to develop. Like a seed in the ground, it sprouts in its own time. "Friendship is a plant of slow

---

4. Maria Cole with Louie Robinson, *Nat King Cole: An Intimate Biography* (New York: William Morrow, 1971), p. 82.

growth," observed George Washington. Like a child in a womb, a new friendship slowly begins to take shape.

Ben Franklin and a number of his most ingenious acquaintances formed "a club of mutual improvement" which they called the Junto. Every Friday night the group of friends met to discuss points of morals, politics, or philosophy. The Junto Club met for almost four decades and, in Franklin's words, "was the best school of philosophy, morality, and politics that then existed in the province." Members inspired each other to read, write, and speak in public. They became excellent scholars and speakers, while remaining close friends without interruption for forty years.

When friendship begins to grow the friends gradually become aware that something new has been born. Awareness of this movement—from acquaintanceship, to casual friendship, to close friendship—brings a deep sense of satisfaction.

New emotional and intellectual experiences help deepen friendships. Thus, husbands and wives, brothers and sisters, colleagues, and other people who share many dimensions may develop third-self friendships.

Winston Churchill and Franklin Delano Roosevelt enjoyed an intimate friendship and often flew to Casablanca to spend a week's holiday alone together.

"I love these Americans," Winston Churchill once confided to his physician, after an all-day auto trip to Marrakesh with Roosevelt and some of his assistants (who were there to help the crippled President).

> That night there was a family dinner party, when the President and the Prime Minister made little affectionate speeches to each other, and Winston sang.[5]

Next morning, when Roosevelt was scheduled to depart from Casablanca, Churchill overslept. According to his physician,

5. Moran, *Churchill: Taken from the Diaries of Lord Moran* (Boston: Houghton Mifflin Company, 1966), p. 90.

he appeared at the door in bedroom slippers and "a most flamboyant dressing gown, covered with red dragons. He got into the President's car in this gay garment and drove with him to the airfield." [6]

Created by the people involved, a third self usually emerges displaying some qualities of each friend and a uniqueness of its own. Some third selves are warming, healing, pleasant relationships. Others are more intense, fiery, explosive or exciting.

In each third self the friends are drawn together. Externally, friends may appear quite different; internally, there is usually an essential likeness. For example, both friends may enjoy working hard, or working casually, or they may both enjoy physical activities, or passive ones. In any case, their peculiar combination of similarities and differences allows a unique third self of friendship to emerge.

Blocking and Unblocking the Process

At any point in the process, the development of a friendship may stop or be delayed. Many experiences of we-ness do not develop into even casual friendships and many casual friendships go no further.

New England poet Emily Dickinson admired a preacher, the Reverend Charles Wadsworth. They met and chatted on two or three occasions, and carried on an intermittent correspondence. While Emily deeply wished to develop their acquaintanceship into a we-ness and even into a close relationship, the Reverend Mr. Wadsworth did not seem to share her wish. For over twenty years she remained open and eager for friendship; many of her poems were about him. After her death, his photo and a privately printed book of his sermons were found among her few guarded possessions. [7]

Friendship may be described as a very special kind of we-

6. *Ibid.*, p. 90.
7. Louis Untermeyer, "Emily Dickinson," *Makers of the Modern World* (New York: Simon & Schuster, 1955).

ness. It is a relationship that has the potential of becoming a third self, between people who actually experience the world as a "we" in ways they freely choose and define.

If a friendship is to deepen, friends must become known to each other. Yet, in a competitive and mobile society, people often feel "required" to wear a mask or to pretend to be what they are not. In the words of psychotherapist Sidney M. Jourard,

> We are role players, every one of us. We say that we feel things we do not feel. We say that we did things we did not do. We say that we believe things we do not believe. We pretend that we are loving when we are full of hostility. We pretend that we are calm and indifferent when we actually are trembling with anxiety and fear.[8]

Close friendships require that people change this pattern. Instead of pretense, self-disclosure is necessary. This opens up a blocked friendship-process.

In one of his poems, Walt Whitman treats the theme of being without friends and, using the analogy of a solitary oak tree, he states his choice.

> Without any companion it grew there,
>   uttering joyous leaves of dark green.
> And its look, rude, unbending, lusting, made
>   me think of myself,
> But I wondered how it could utter joyous
>   leaves,
> Standing alone there, without its friend, its
>   lover near—for I knew I could not.

To Tame a Friend

Each person is entitled to be a "self" and to keep that self private when not yet ready to disclose it. But when they are ready to make friends, it helps to disclose the self. Self-disclosure makes friendship possible. "I feel so safe in your

---

8. Sidney M. Jourard, with Ardis Whitman, "The Fear That Cheats Us of Love," *Redbook Magazine*, October 1971, p. 83.

"Self disclosure is necessary in friendship"

presence," says the friend, "that I am willing to tell you things I wouldn't tell anyone else."

Self-disclosure allows people to know themselves and to understand others.

For the fox in *The Little Prince*, the process involves taming.

"One only understands the things that one tames," said the fox to the Little Prince, who was in search of a friend.

"If you want a friend, tame me."

"What must I do, to tame you?" asked the little prince.

"You must be very patient," replied the fox.

"First you will sit down at a little distance from me—like that—in the grass. I shall look at you out of the corner of my eye, and you will say nothing. Words are the source of misunderstandings. But you will sit a little closer to me, every day." [9]

And thus the Little Prince tamed the fox.

9. Antoine de Saint-Exupery, *The Little Prince* (New York: Harcourt, Brace & Co., 1943), p. 67.

4

The Life of Friendship

Seedlings turn overnight to sunflowers,
Blossoming even as we gaze.

"SUNRISE, SUNSET,"
Fiddler on the Roof

The Birth of Friendship

The original matrix for friendship is in the home where a child's first bonds of love are formed with mother and father, then with other family members.

"Mommy, stay with me." "Daddy, take me with you." "My brother is my friend." "Hey, can I play with you?" "When is Grandpa going to come and tell more stories?"

Benjamin Spock claims that relationships with parents are crucial to later relationships with friends.[1]

Irene, first child of scientists Marie and Pierre Curie, used to enjoy the friendship of her mother and father every evening at home. But after the Curies won the Nobel Prize for their discovery of radioactivity, their whole way of life changed. And they saw Irene less and less.

Because of their fame, the Curies had to go out night after

1. Benjamin Spock, "How Children Learn to Make Friends," *Redbook Magazine*, November 1972.

night, to give lectures or attend banquets and receptions held in their honor.

"Don't go," pleaded Irene one evening when her parents, dressed in formal evening wear, came to give the child a kiss at the front door. "Stay with me. You never stay with me anymore."

"I wish we could," Madame Curie sighed unhappily. "The President of the Republic sent us an invitation. It wasn't polite for us to refuse, dear."

"He has no right," the girl pouted. "He has no right to take you away."

Her father put his hand on her hair. "The child speaks the truth." [2]

Children whose parents spend plenty of time with them are likely to learn how to relate to people and to form friendships in later life.

Children who are unbefriended at home may stand around at the playground or at school feeling awkward and excluded, not knowing what to do or say, or how to meet other children.

Salvador Dali's parents hardly ever played with him as a child. They expected him to live up to their glorified memories of his dead brother. Unable to fulfill their expectations, the young boy became hyperactive and even sadistic. According to a biographer,

> He kicked his sister's head as if it were a football. At five he threw another child over a railing and nearly killed him. He bit into a putrescent bat; he broke the doctor's glasses; he trod upon a classmate's violin. By the time he was adolescent he was so eccentric in his manner and dress that he was stoned when he went to the movies. He had no satisfying relationships with the boys and girls in his immediate neighborhood.[3]

2. Robin McKown, *She Lived for Science: Irene Joliot-Curie* (New York: Julian Messner, 1961), p. 18.
3. Victor and Mildred Goertzel, *Cradles of Eminence* (Boston: Little, Brown, 1961), pp. 210–211.

Dali went on to become a famous modern artist, eventually overcoming, though not totally, his difficulties in relating to others. Among his few friends today, according to one story, are his wife, Gala, his agent and confidant—and his two pet ocelots.[4]

Childhood Friendships

Friendship is a developmental process which goes through many stages. Children change their views of friendship and learn new patterns of relating from time to time as they grow older.[5]

For example, two-year-olds characteristically play in the same room but not together. One may be absorbed in building blocks, the other in toy cars. They seem hardly to notice each other. During this early stage, children seem to prefer parallel play to cooperative play.

For very young children, friendship is often defined by playing in the same room or area. And sharing means that a friend "gives *me* things."

Around the age of three the skill of sharing and playing *with* someone else begins to develop. At this "together" stage, children cooperate in building a sandcastle or a house of blocks. They discover simple cooperative games like playing house, playing school or jumping rope.

Nursery schools provide a matrix for the "together" stage, offering children opportunities to play together, care for others, enjoy others, and make others happy.

At about this age children develop affectionate feelings toward

4. Robert Wernick, "Dali's Dollars," *Life,* July 24, 1970.
5. Canadian psychologist John J. LaGaipa recently began researching "a developmental-cognitive approach to the study of friendship in children," based on the ideas of Jean Piaget and Lawrence Kohlberg. With Brian J. Bigelow he delivered a paper on "The Development of Childhood Friendship Expectations" at the Canadian Psychological Association meetings in Montreal, 1972.

grownups as well as other children. They may strike up friendly relationships with a mail carrier, with an older neighbor who is willing to talk to them, or with an uncle who plays ball with them whenever he visits.

Associated Press columnist Hal Boyle was famous for the way he related to families. Friends at the office labeled him "the world's best weekend guest."

"He arrived with a bag full of compassion and charm for the hostess, and candy or gum for the kids," recalled colleague Saul Pett. "He also came with a supply of beguiling abstractions, or 'murkyisms' as we called them in the office." Children loved his murkyisms.

Once, with Pett's youngest on his knee, Boyle said, "Sukey, remember one thing. Be kind to your dear and true to your always."

She stared back at him and said, "Mr. Boyle, that doesn't make any sense." And together Sukey and Boyle laughed and hugged each other.[6]

Through grownups and other children, youngsters learn a variety of relationship styles. Some involve activities, others conversation, play, learning, exploring, or just being together. The more meaningful and varied these childhood relationships are, the likelier the child will be to form deep friendships in later life.

One of Margaret Mead's oldest friends once said to her, "In my house I was a child. In your family's house I was a person."

The Chum Period

Psychiatrist Harry Stack Sullivan is known for his study of the ways in which interpersonal relations affect personality growth. He claimed that real friendship does not happen until

6. Saul Pett, "Unforgettable Hal Boyle," *Reader's Digest*, October 1974, pp. 118–119.

the chum period, beginning at about age eight and lasting until about twelve. Until then, he believed, children do not form true friendships but merely imitate patterns of affection and relating they learned from others.

The chum period, occurring before heterosexual functioning begins, is a time when children tend to select "friends" from those of the same sex. It is also a time when they develop the capacity to care for others as much as for themselves. Young people who enjoy healthy chum experiences are likelier to trust special relationships and seek out close friendships during adolescence. If the chum experience is missing, says Sullivan, young people may not develop strong heterosexual attachments later.[7]

Classic stories such as *Little Women* and *The Bobbsey Twins* develop examples of the chum period among girls.

The Adventures of Tom Sawyer and *The Adventures of Huckleberry Finn*, both by Mark Twain, spin out delightful stories of perhaps the most famous boy chums in history. Young Tom Sawyer seldom did anything alone. There was always a friend with whom he could share his joys or his burdens. One day Tom felt so rejected that a "life of crime" seemed the only alternative left to him.

> Just at this point he met his soul's sworn comrade, Joe Harper —hard-eyed, and with evidently a great and dismal purpose in his heart. Plainly, here were "two souls with but a single thought."

Joe had just been whipped by his mother for drinking some cream which he had never tasted and knew nothing about.

Tom and Joe found deep empathy in each other. Each knew how the other felt. They agreed to share their life and fortune in eternal friendship.

> As the two boys walked sorrowing along, they made a new compact to stand by each other and be brothers and never

7. Discussed in Rollo May, *Love and Will* (New York: W. W. Norton, 1969), p. 316.

separate till death relieved them of their troubles. Then they began to lay their plans.[8]

As children mature into the chum period, their friendships begin to lose some of the egocentric flavor of earlier relationships, and to grow in empathy, "or the ability to take others' points of view into account." [9]

In his experiments with rhesus monkeys, Harry Harlow confirmed that early companionship is also necessary for animals. He discovered that monkeys in childhood who were not allowed to play with others and make friends did not function adequately and affectionately in their later sexual lives. For animals as well as humans, friendships in childhood seem essential to later maturity.[10]

Many friendships, born in youth, last throughout life.

Elizabeth Taylor met actor Roddy McDowall when as children they both played in a film called *Lassie*. Almost thirty years later she referred to him as "just about my oldest friend —and really the perfect friend."

David Eisenhower and Julie Nixon knew each other from childhood, attended neighboring colleges and eventually married.

When Roger Staubach, star quarterback for the Dallas Cowboys, was a small boy in St. John's Catholic Grammar School, he sat in the second row behind a little girl named Marianne Hoobler. To tease her, he sometimes tried to push her desk closer to the front of the room. Marianne would brace her feet on the floor and push back. They became good friends and years later sealed their friendship in marriage.[11]

8. Mark Twain, *The Adventures of Tom Sawyer* (New York: Harper & Row, 1903), p. 112.

9. John J. LaGaipa and Brian J. Bigelow, "The Development of Childhood Friendship Expectations."

10. Harry Harlow, "Affection in Primates," *Discovery*, January 1966.

11. Marshall and Sue Burchard, *Sports Hero Roger Staubach* (New York: G. P. Putnam's Sons, 1973), p. 9.

Changing Friendship Patterns

Boys and girls of grammar school age usually rate parents, other children, and teachers as the most significant people in their lives—in that order.

During these years for the first time, peer relationships—chums, comrades, classmates, buddies, friends—become important. The center of attention for friends at this age is still, as in early childhood, play and doing things together. Boys make friends with other boys, and girls with other girls.[12]

Beginning around age twelve, patterns begin to change. At the first onrush of biological maturation, boys often turn away from girls with derision and contempt. Girls, by contrast, tend to foster romantic thoughts and fantasies about boys.

By the time boys and girls reach early adolescence, usually in the junior high school years, opposite-sex adolescents are added to their list of significant people.[13]

Elizabeth Taylor was a daydreamer in her early teens. The motion picture *National Velvet*, made when she was thirteen years old, launched her career in film. Even though she was at home on the MGM lot, she was still romantically fascinated by "movie stars" and used to carry an autograph book with her when she went to lunch at MGM's commissary.

Sometimes, too, Elizabeth would daydream with two girls who lived on her block in Beverly Hills. The friends called themselves The Three Musketeers.

12. J. M. Tanner, "Sequence, Tempo, and Individual Variation in Growth and Development of Boys and Girls Aged Twelve to Sixteen" in *12 to 16: Early Adolescence*, ed. Jerome Kagan and Robert Coles (New York: W. W. Norton, 1972), p. 26.

13. Of course, in many cases heterosexual interest and experimentation may begin earlier than adolescence. Magazines and television programs that tend to stimulate sexual curiosity are universally available to young people. Among certain personality types, sexual experimentation begun before adolescence may remain a lifelong pattern.

Like most little girls we were very romantic and had our own imaginary boyfriends. We'd make up plays for ourselves and make up stories, and of course I was really *in*, because I could say, "Well, I know Van Johnson, so Van Johnson is going to be *my* boyfriend today. But I'll let you have him tomorrow." [14]

At this age, according to some child analysts, boys typically direct their energies outward. They like to *do* things, to master skills and gain control of the outside world. They may want to be strong and have powerful muscles. Basketballs and catcher's mitts may be primary points of interest. Mechanical skills and handyman talents may be discovered and developed as ways of controlling things. Boys often choose friends who will facilitate and support this dominance over things.

In contrast, girls like Elizabeth Taylor's Three Musketeers find outlets for their energies in deep-felt emotions that are focused on boys, either in fact or fantasy. Many girls' feelings toward boys tend to be a blend of romantic tenderness, possessiveness, envy and anger.[15]

For a variety of reasons, friendships among young adolescents are often exploitative. To some youngsters friends are for dominating or possessing; to others, friends act as protection and support against enemies. For still others, friends serve to enhance the emerging "self."

Adolescent Friends

In early adolescence, boys and girls begin to acquire ownership of their bodies in new ways, and to experience the ecstasy of a "self." For many young people, this is a momentous and memorable time. It is also a period of tensions—

14. Elizabeth Taylor, *Elizabeth Taylor: An Informal Memoir* (New York: Harper & Row, 1965), pp. 18–19.
15. Peter Blos, "The Child Analyst Looks at the Young Adolescent," in *12 to 16: Early Adolescence*, ed. Jerome Kagan and Robert Coles, pp. 59–61.

sexual, social and emotional. Childhood comes to a close. Adolescence intensifies two familiar challenges: *achievement* ("measuring up," "making it," "being able to make the grade") and *acceptance* ("being liked," "being a part of things," "finding friends").

Junior high schools are frequently scenes of intense friendship groupings. When Thomas Jefferson was of junior high age he attended James Maury's school, where he faced the challenges of achievement and acceptance. The building was just a log house, and there were only five students in his class, but for Jefferson, the school was a font of friendship. Three of his classmates, who later rose to prominence in Virginia, became his long-lasting friends.[16]

Youngsters without friends in junior high are a painful sight. "In our school people don't associate with freaks, brains, or wallflowers," explained one student.

Because of social pressure, young people who are shy, sensitive, or late-bloomers can be hurt before they have time to blossom as friends. In high school "friends become more important than anything," a fifteen-year-old boy recalled.

> You had to have a lot of friends. That was more important than anything else. My mother would say, "Are you going out to play now?" And I'd say, "No. I don't play. I want to be with my friends."

A fifteen-year-old girl wrote to a magazine columnist:

> My mother keeps talking to me about boys and my social life. She arranges parties and dates for me with her friends' sons. I find them boring. What I really love is horseback riding, especially jumping. When I tell my mother what I really like, she gets angry and upset. That makes me feel there is something wrong with me.

Young people are expected to initiate relationships, but they also learn to explain and deal with possible or actual rejection

16. Dumas Malone, *Jefferson the Virginian* (Boston: Little, Brown, 1948), pp. 40–42.

by others. At almost every turn, the budding "self" faces possible rejection.[17]

Many young people also worry about newly discovered emotions like anger, aggressiveness and possessiveness. "What if I really let my feelings out?" "What if I say something to embarrass myself?" "What if I can't control my reactions?" "What if my friends won't like me anymore?" "What if they don't stay around to make sure that nothing happens to me?"

Conflicting urges are typical during high school years. Wanting to reach out in friendship *and* holding back are both reflected in sixteen-year-old Tina's words.

> When I love someone and want to know him better, I am afraid to tell him of my feelings for fear that his reaction will disappoint me. This would shatter all the fantasies I had while loving this person before I told him. So, I may stifle my feelings of love because I don't want to handle the disappointment of being refused the real love that I would eventually ask for.[18]

Many young people can identify with Tina's fear, and with the collision of values happening within her.

Parents often don't understand that for young people, school with its demands for academic competence often takes second place to the need to have friends.

Romanticism in Friendship

Romance is characteristic of many teen-age friendships; friends are loved intensely and possessively; they need to be in each other's presence continually. Like Romeo and Juliet, they cannot live without each other. Friendship is seen through rose-colored glasses that distort reality in glorious ways.

Romantic friends—whether same-sex or opposite-sex—see each

---

17. Jerome Kagan, "A Conception of Early Adolescence," in *12 to 16: Early Adolescence*, pp. 97–98.
18. Tina de Varon, "Growing Up," in *12 to 16: Early Adolescence*, p. 342.

other as "divine," without fault and without equal. They use expressions like "I almost worship her" or "He's so perfect I'd do *anything* for him."

Young Victoria, barely twenty-one, but already queen of England for three years, was standing at the top of the staircase at Windsor Castle to receive her cousins, Prince Albert and Prince Ernest. She knew that Albert was good looking; everyone spoke of how handsome he was, but her romantic heart was not prepared for the reality.

"It was with some emotion that I beheld Albert—who is *beautiful!*" she wrote in her diary. And again,

> Albert really is quite charming, and so excessively handsome, such beautiful blue eyes, an exquisite nose, and such a pretty mouth with delicate mustachios and slight but very slight whiskers; a beautiful figure, broad in the shoulders and a fine waist; my heart is quite *going*. . . . [19]

By the next day her heart was completely gone. She first informed Albert by note that he "made a very favorable impression on her" and later told him personally that he was her choice for husband and Prince Consort. He agreed.

> We embraced each other over and over again, and he was *so* kind, *so* affectionate; Oh! to *feel* I was, and am, loved by *such* an Angel as Albert was *too great delight to describe!* He is perfection; perfection in every way—in beauty—in everything! I told him I was quite unworthy of him and kissed his dear hand.[20]

Teen-age friendships often become so intense that the friends may generate an unreal atmosphere around themselves, preventing them from seeing anyone or anything but each other.

Because of their rapidly developing bodies and a new awareness of sexual feelings, they may experiment with homosexual

19. *RA Queen Victoria's Journal*, 11–14 October 1839, quoted in Cecil Woodham-Smith *Queen Victoria: From Her Birth to the Death of the Prince Consort* (New York: Knopf, 1972), p. 187.
20. *Ibid.*

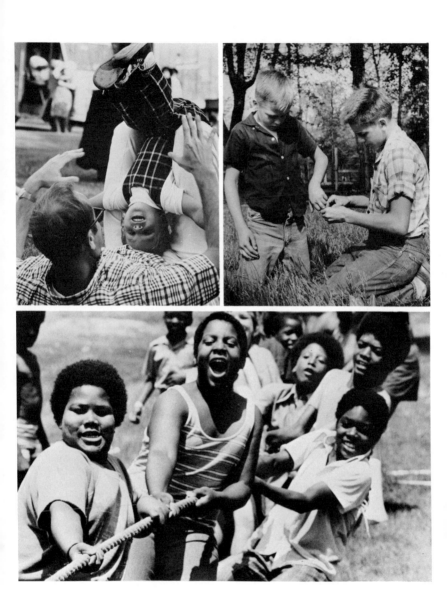

 "Friendship is a developmental process"

❧ "Some friendships, born in youth,
last throughout life"

as well as heterosexual relationships. The experimentation can lead to important decisions regarding sex in later life.

If people enter marriage with a Viewpoint 1 teen-age expectancy, their romanticized marriages may end quickly. Seldom do couples "live happily ever after" as promised in fairy tales and "romance" magazines. Instead, the glow fades and soon the honeymoon is over. Complaints become more and more frequent: "You don't seem to love me anymore" or "You used to spend a lot of time with me, but now you're always busy."

Even after bad experiences in purely romantic attachments, some grownups do not learn from their mistakes. Instead, they continue to long for someone new who will sweep them off their feet and be the answer to all their dreams. Such romantic dreamers may become involved time after time in heavy "affairs" searching for the "mystical oneness" they once romantically experienced.

Maturing Friendships

While intense romanticism may be normal in adolescent friendships, it distorts and destroys friendships among adults. Maturing friendships that have healthily passed through possible periods of romanticism are marked by a spirit of freedom and love.

Most "we" relationships follow customary patterns. Society—either explicitly or implicitly—prescribes certain ways of acting for parents, spouses and children. In traditional "we" relationships, people usually do what is expected of them. According to custom, parents take care of their children; a husband and wife live in the same dwelling; children adopt their father's surname; hobby groups are concerned with their hobbies; political groups work for particular issues or candidates.

Although people do not always carry out what society expects, they *know* what is expected of them. Even if they protest or get angry, they usually keep their behavior within expected or prescribed limits.

The qualities that most clearly distinguish a maturing third self of friendship from other "we" relationships are *freedom* and *love*. In the words of Andrew Greeley:

> When we come in contact with our friend we enter into a different environment where the air we breathe is more pure, the sounds we hear are sharper, the colors we see more dramatic, and the ideas we think quicker and more inciteful. The physical environment, of course, is not different at all, but the psychosocial environment is completely different, because now we are in a situation not only where we are free to be ourselves but where we have no choice.[21]

In a third self, friends are not forced to do what they should do. There are no societal "shoulds" in true friendship. Mature friends do what they feel they must out of a deep sense of mutual loving commitment. A third self may be recognized by the fact that it is freely created and its activity is freely and lovingly defined by the people involved.

"Every friendship," observed Ladislas Örsy, "is unique and does not conform to a precise pattern."

Friendship's cement is the freedom to *be*, not just to do. The words "friend" and "free" grew out of each other. The Old English word *freo* meant free; not in bondage; noble; glad. The Old English word *freon* means to love, and the word *freoud* becomes our modern English "friend."

The third self grows in an environment of freedom and love. When people freely create new loving expectancies in their relationships, their "we-ness" develops from a casual friendship into a third self.

The Robert Browning-Elizabeth Barrett love story began very casually. Though they knew each other's poetry and had friends and acquaintances in common, they did not meet until he was thirty-two and she was thirty-eight.

Their almost daily letters to each other—nearly six hundred

21. Andrew M. Greeley, *The Friendship Game* (Garden City, N.Y.: Doubleday Image Books, 1971), p. 110.

all together—reveal the third self that developed between these two creative people, sometimes struggling, almost obsessively, through misunderstandings. Describing their relationship, Elizabeth wrote: ". . . our two souls stand up erect and strong, face to face, silent, drawing nigh and nigher." [22]

In the intensity of their love and friendship, their unique identities were never lost. Instead, their closeness created what they described as a "fire" between them. For them, this fire was a new life (a third self) from which they both drew strength. They could say to each other, "I do not think of thee—I am too near thee." [23]

One freedom often overlooked in friendship is the privilege of forming other third selves with different people. People can enjoy several third selves, each one quite different from the others and not necessarily compatible. In each third self, people are free to behave differently and in ways agreed upon by the friends involved.

During her university years at the Sorbonne, Simone de Beauvoir, feminist author of *The Second Sex*, made close friendships with three inseparable male companions: Sartre, Nizan, and Herbaud.

Her autobiography describes her first initiation to the three comrades in Sartre's apartment.

> I was feeling a bit scared when I entered Sartre's room; there were books all over the place, cigarette ends in all the corners and the air was thick with tobacco smoke. Sartre greeted me in a worldly manner; he was smoking a pipe. Nizan, who said nothing, had a cigarette stuck in the corner of his one-sided smile and was quizzing me through his pebble lenses, with an air of thinking more than he cared to say. All day long, petrified with fear, I annotated the "metaphysical treatise" and in the evening Herbaud took me home.[24]

22. Elizabeth Barrett Browning, *Sonnets from the Portuguese*, Sonnet XXII.
23. *Ibid.*, Sonnet XXX.
24. Simone de Beauvoir, *Memoirs of a Dutiful Daughter* (New York: Harper & Row, 1959), p. 334.

Within a few days, her fear subsided and she learned to feel at home with the trio. Her friendship with each man had a slightly different emphasis. With André Herbaud she was affectionate and trusting. "He has a kind of intelligence that goes straight to my heart," she wrote in her diary. Of the three, usually Herbaud escorted her home and often took her out for coffee, dinner or a holiday. From him she received reassurance. "I am delighted that you should be getting along so well with the comrades," said Herbaud to her.

The relationship with Nizan, who was married, emphasized classwork and intellectual research. A social dimension developed later when Nizan and his wife and Sartre and Simone enjoyed holidays together in the country.

Her deepest friendship developed with Jean-Paul Sartre. In her journal she wrote:

> Sartre corresponded exactly to the dream-companion I had longed for since I was fifteen: he was the double in whom I found all my burning aspirations raised to the pitch of incandescence. I should always be able to share everything with him. When I left him at the beginning of August, I knew that he would never go out of my life again.[25]

Simone de Beauvoir and Jean-Paul Sartre chose not to marry yet remained most intimate, often inseparable, friends throughout life.

Breaking Up Friendships

While breaking up a friendship is almost always painful, and should be a last resort, after every attempt has been made to keep it healthy, sometimes it is necessary to end a friendship.

"When a friendship is no longer enjoyable on any level," said psychologist Daniel A. Sugarman, "surely when it is destructive, it's time to cut the ties." [26]

25. *Ibid.*, p. 345.
26. Daniel A. Sugarman, Ph.D. and Rolaine Hochstein, *The Seventeen Guide to Knowing Yourself* (New York: Macmillan, 1967), p. 35.

The need to break up friendships occurs often, in most cases because friends simply outgrow each other, or find new interests and follow different pathways. These relationships dissolve naturally for lack of mutual nourishment.

In other cases, friends once admired seem in the light of new ideas and values to be less admirable. "I used to think she was so great," said Helene. "I always wanted to be with her. Now I realize that she's a snob and wants only to climb the social ladder."

Friendships, like plants, may die naturally, but sometimes they need to be pulled up forcibly by the roots. This is true of destructive relationships of which a master-slave relationship is a familiar example.

"I sometimes feel that Sara leads me around by a leash," explained Cindy. "She's always telling me, 'Do this! Do that!' I sometimes feel like I'm a dog whose whole reason for living is to make her happy."

A relationship is destructive when one friend displays a sense of superiority, habitually criticizes, disparages, oppresses, punishes and demeans the other.

Rhoda often threw painful darts at Liam in a sadistic way, making comments like, "Why don't you get a good haircut?" "Look at those sloppy trousers!" "Why read that book, you'll never understand it." "You'll probably *never* learn how to act in front of people." "I don't think you'll ever amount to anything."

Both Cindy and Liam need to realize that their destructive relationships can never do them any good, and to close the curtain on them.

The Death of Friendship

The death of friendship can be as painful as the death of an individual.

"I can't take it. She won't even talk to me," sobbed Elsie, a forty-year-old teacher. "I thought we were friends. Now it turns out we're almost enemies, just because I was given the job she wanted."

"Life will never be the same," wrote Walter in his diary. "The sunshine's gone behind a cloud since she moved away." He and Margaret used to play chess every day.

Because a third self of friendship possesses a life in process, it can die because one friend—or both—has changed radically. With no common interest, no bond, there is no longer a matrix of friendship.

Sometimes people who were friends in the matrix of high school, or of a hobby or job, meet after years of separation. After sharing memories of past relationships or "catching up" on what's happened since their last meeting, they find themselves with nothing left to say. They still *like* each other and call each other "friend," but the third self of friendship no longer exists.

A friendship may die also because there has been stagnation among relating partners. Everyone knows of clubs or families or groups who have been doing "the same old thing" year after year. Nothing new, nothing fresh, nothing vital.

These relationships are reduced to expected patterns of behavior, rituals executed with little or no loving freedom. Without expressions of love and freedom, a third self dies for lack of nourishment.

In the play *Five Finger Exercise* a lonely college man, Clyde, tries desperately to enrich his relationship with his father and mother.

> Why can't we be important to each other? Why can't we ever come back into the room and be new to each other? Why doesn't a night's sleep lying all those dark hours with ourselves forgotten and then coming alive again, why doesn't it ever change us? Give us new things to see—new things to say too: not just "Eat your eggs," or "You were in late"—the old dreariness.[27]

27. Peter Shafer, *Five Finger Exercise* (New York: Harcourt, Brace, Jovanovich, 1958), pp. 57, 58, 107.

A friendship may die from misunderstandings over loyalty. Words and actions may be perceived in different ways, even by two friends.

"I told my wife we went to the Playboy Club," said one young executive to his friend.

"You stupid nut," replied the other. "When the story gets back to *my* wife, I'm in for it. Why did you ever tell on us?"

One friend interpreted his action as acceptable, the other as betrayal.

Misunderstanding created a problem between Kathy and Joan, who had been friends for many years. Joan reported the splintering event as follows:

> Kathy was married to my brother. They divorced last year at the same time I was getting my divorce. We had always been friends so decided that we needed something to make us feel good, so we went to Puerto Vallarta together. One night we went to a discothèque together with one guy who had taken us several times.

> Always before the guy had danced with both of us, but this night the two of them went off and left me sitting alone at a table with just a bunch of chairs. It was a very fancy jet-set discothèque, and I cannot tell you what a difficult night that was. I didn't know that she had left and I kept waiting for them to come back.

> The whole seventh-grade syndrome of being rejected and not being asked to dance and having all these jet-set type people see that I had failed and that my very best friend did that to me was an awful lot of stuff to go through.

> Well, I finally realized what had happened and left. The next day she did not want to deal with it at all. She pretended it didn't happen. It was a really horrendous experience for me.

> I would have thought that she would not have done anything like this but the truth is she deserted me when she left and that was rough. We never straightened it out because she didn't want to talk about it. Something is missing in our relationship now.

Undying Friendships

A change of job, home or interest is not necessarily a sign to drop old friends, still less to turn former friends into enemies.

Friends are worth the effort it takes to make them, and it is wise to think carefully before breaking a relationship. Better to invent formulas for mellowing friendships than for splitting them. In the words of Ben Franklin, "Be slow in choosing a friend, slower in changing."

In anyone's life, there is room for stimulating new friendships, and for old ones which, like old shoes, are comfortable and satisfying. Old friends become more and more precious as the years go on. In the poetry of Eunice Tietjens,

> Beautiful and rich is an old friendship . . .
> Smooth as aged wine, or sheen on tapestry
> Where light has lingered, intimate and long.

The acting careers of sisters Dorothy and Lillian Gish, which began in the 1920s, moved through the entire cycle of American show business, from road companies to television. The sisters were also close friends. Their friendship grew and mellowed in a lifetime voyage together through almost two hundred movies and over sixty stage productions.

They learned to count by watching the man in the box office and to read schoolbooks under their mother's tutelage in dressing rooms and day coaches. Together they started a tradition in film acting. Film critic Brooks Atkinson described these sister-friends as saturated with goodwill and with not a drop of vanity.[28]

A third self of friendship may transcend distance and time. Many engaged couples or husbands and wives during wartime maintained a vital third-self friendship from opposite

28. Brooks Atkinson, "Critic at Large," *New York Times*, December 27, 1960.

ends of the world. There are friends who are able to maintain a healthy third self through months and years of separation. Whenever they manage to get together, they simply "pick up where they left off."

Across the Barrier of Death

Third-self friendships do not have to die, even when one of the friends has died.

Many people report strong bonds stretching across the abyss of death. Contact is maintained through photographs, recalling fond memories, holding imaginary conversations with the dead person, and keeping in touch with the dead friend's relatives, children, family and other friends.

As one woman expressed it, "For me a deep friendship doesn't seem to die when a friend dies, rather the friendship seems caught up in some kind of cosmic dimension."

Doris Day called Jacqueline Susann her closest friend, and still does, even though Jackie has died. Their friendship began when Jackie sent a letter saying that their pet poodles looked exactly alike. Doris wrote back, and before long they were exchanging letters several times a month.

"One day she came to the Coast," Doris recalled. "It was as if we had known each other forever."

They even invented crazy names to call each other. Doris was called Clara Bixby and Jackie was renamed Opal Mandelbaum. From then on, they used these new names with each other instead of their real names.

When Doris heard of Jackie's terminal cancer, she flew to New York intending to remain at her bedside until the end, but she was called back to Los Angeles to testify in court. Back in Los Angeles on the day of the funeral, Doris recalled,

> I looked at the clock. It was the time the funeral services began in New York. I closed my eyes and there was Opal, radiant. She appeared to me with a man I supposed was her father.

She was smiling and said, "Clara, I'm fine. You were absolutely right. Life is eternal." [29]

Her eyes were moist when she related the story. "Opal is still with me," she said. "She always will be."

The following account of friendship that transcends death was reported by a woman who is a personal friend of the authors.

"Six months after my grandfather died," she said, "I was talking with Harry, the man who had been his most trusted friend and employee for more than 25 years."

In an intent and quiet voice Harry, who always called her grandfather "Captain," told the following:

Early one morning about three weeks ago, I saw Captain walking from his porch across the way to his carpentry shop just the way he used to each morning. I thought I'd mislaid my wits. Then I thought, "Everything's all right. He's not dead after all!" I found myself walking towards him and saying, "Good morning, Captain" the way I always did and he answered, "It's a fine morning, Harry." Since then, I see him often in the early mornings. I know he's not alive, but yet to me he is. I see him. We speak to each other.

According to priest-psychiatrist Ignace Lepp, friendship enables people to "see with different eyes, not only our own lives, but the entire universe." Friendship, wrote Lepp, is "the most universal and, in our opinion, the noblest of all forms of interhuman communication." [30]

Friendship is the relationship most capable of dissolving loneliness; it guarantees happiness and joy even in the midst of the worst tribulations. It is least dependent upon mutations of flesh and surface beauty.

"True friendship between two people," wrote Plato, "is infinite and immortal."

29. Rex Reed, "Doris Day Remembers: 'My Friend Jackie,'" *Ladies Home Journal*, January 1975, p. 58.

30. Ignace Lepp, *The Ways of Friendship: A Psychological Exploration of Man's Most Valuable Relationship* (New York: Macmillan, 1966), p. 21.

~~§ 5 §~~

The Expectancies of Friendship

> The costliness of keeping friends does not lie in
> what one does for them but in what one, out of
> consideration for them, refrains from doing.
>   HENRIK IBSEN

Qualities of Friendship

Third-self friendship grows best in an environment of freedom. It has the potential for unboundedness, an unlimited way
of experiencing the world. Yet, even in friendship, expectations exist.

Expectancies that seem to influence the process and life of
most friendships include *availability, doing things together,
caring, honesty, confidentiality, loyalty, understanding and
empathy*.

The first two, *availability* and *doing things together*, are particularly important in initial stages of friendship. They are so
basic in fact that most friends simply presume their presence
in a close relationship.

Caring, honesty, confidentiality and *loyalty* are also common.
They provide a norm or structure for most friendship. Poets
and philosophers who write about the meaning of friendship
often focus on them. Once a friendship is established, these
four expectancies help keep it alive and well. When they are
violated, the relationship may be disrupted.

The final expectancy, *understanding and empathy*, involves levels of intimacy, acceptance, communication, "being open and real with a person." This expectancy is met in third-self friendships; casual friendships tend to lack it.

As friendships develop, these seven expectancies usually appear. All of them remain important throughout the life of third-self friendship.

Researchers La Gaipa and Bigelow report that, from a developmental psychological point of view, expectancies in the basic category of *doing things together* are frequently mentioned by the youngest friends. Normative expectancies, the second category, begin to occur clearly among fifth and sixth graders. Expectancies dealing with *empathy* are first recognized, as a rule, only around the seventh and eighth grades.[1]

Being Available

Even ancient writers stress the fact that friendship thrives on "presence." Friends need to *be together*.

Bob Dylan was devoted to guitar-playing folk singer Woodie Guthrie. When Guthrie was in the hospital suffering from a severe nerve disease, Dylan came to visit him. "Guthrie was very shaky, he could barely talk, and he was very difficult to look at. But Dylan would sit beside him and play the guitar for him and somehow they communicated."[2]

Often busy friends may have to go out of their way to make a meeting possible. Some friends who are financially able arrange to meet periodically at a halfway spot where they can spend a friendship weekend together. Beforehand, they can make lists of all the things they would like to discuss and do with each other. Preparations for such a weekend heighten the sense of third self.

1. LaGaipa and Bigelow, "The Development of Childhood Friendship Expectations," paper delivered to Canadian Psychological Association, 1972.
2. Anthony Scaduto, *Bob Dylan: An Intimate Biography* (New York: Grosset & Dunlap, 1971), p. 53.

Photographs and films, especially those taken of friends together, act as reminders of events shared.

Physical presence is the most satisfying way of being together, and often there is no substitute for it, but friends must often settle for other ways of expressing presence. The commonest of these are phone calls, letters and gifts.

"Call me," a popular song of a few years ago, expressed the telephone's importance among friends. "Don't be afraid, you can call me/maybe it's late, but just call me."

Leo, a forty-year-old engineer, had enjoyed a close friendship with his cousin Vicki since childhood. Recently, when she was terminally ill, he scribbled a note to her. In it, he recalled some joyful memories important to their third self.

> This is just to let you know I'm thinking of you many times each day.
>
> Also, whenever you're in the mood to speak of important things such as wooden sword duels, gambling joints, midnight water fights, coded messages, transits of Pluto, or any kinda stuff like that there, give me a ring.
>
> Anytime 2 P.M. or 2 A.M. or in between. No matter.
>
> There are few things more fun than an hour or so with an old friend on the phone.
>
> Meanwhile, take care and much love always.

Telephone calls are convenient ways to keep friendships alive. With inexpensive rates during late night and early morning hours and on weekends, the phone provides a relatively inexpensive way to maintain close friendship. At the current weekend phone rate, for about five dollars a friend in New York may talk to a friend in San Francisco for *half an hour!* [3]

Friends usually have each other's unlisted phone numbers and feel entitled to use them. They also know that, if needed, the other person will come to them, physically, if possible,

---

3. Twenty-two cents for the first minute, 16¢ for each additional minute.

but most surely in spirit. In friendship, the feeling is "I want to be available to you and have time for you."

Long before telephones were invented, friends wrote letters when physical presence was impossible. In letters, friends express feelings and experiences, and share things that help maintain contact on the third-self level. However, letters that simply comment about the weather, offer excuses for not writing sooner, or make promises to write a longer letter next time, do little to recharge the friendship circuits.

Anthropologist Margaret Mead, often away from friends for years at a time while doing research, maintained her friendships through letters.

> Writing letters has always been a very real part of my life, especially in the years I have been in the field. For then letters home, letters to colleagues—particularly Ruth Benedict and Geoffrey Gorer—and bulletin letters to a widening circle of family and friends have linked my life to theirs in a way that is fast disappearing from a world in which most people communicate by telephone and, very occasionally, by tape recording.[4]

When physical presence of friends is not possible—and even when it is—friendship may be strengthened and preserved by gifts. Giving gifts, like letter writing, is an art.

James M. Dixon, real estate broker and husband of psychic Jeanne Dixon, is not a man of many words. Instead, he shows his tenderness by frequently giving Jeanne small gifts.

> Every evening I find a deep-red rose lying on my pillow, placed there by Jimmy as a token of his love. If red roses are not available, then he may switch to a soft pink one, but it is always a rose. He started this early in our marriage and has never forgotten.[5]

The many simple gifts Jimmy gave to Jeanne through the years helped to strengthen their friendship and life together.

---

4. Margaret Mead, *Blackberry Winter: My Earlier Years* (New York: William Morrow, 1972), p. 81.
5. Jeanne Dixon, *My Life and Prophecies* (New York: William Morrow, 1969), p. 22.

Gifts need not be costly or frequent. More important are the right gift at the right time and the gift that reveals the giver's heart.

A traveling journalist once said, "One of the happiest memories in my friendship with Bill was when he gave me a fifteen-cent yellow plastic pencil sharpener, the kind kids get in their pencil boxes when they first go to school. I carry it on my travels to cover news events, and whenever I use it, it brings Bill's smiling face to mind, and reminds me of our friendship."

Being Together

Many friendships begin between people who play or work together. *Doing* things together also provides times for friends to *be* together.

"Let's do something tonight." "I found a good idea for our garden project." "Let's do our homework together." "How about a vacation together?" It is a continual wish of friends to do things together, as a way of keeping relationships alive and well.

Organizations such as the Boy Scouts, Girl Scouts, 4-H clubs and Little Leagues are designed to introduce children to each other and suggest things they might do together. Grownups also organize groups to do things together such as bowling teams, bridge clubs and dancing groups. Some groups like the Sierra Club and the Red Cross do humanitarian things. Sometimes the things friends do are religious, political, economic or educational.

All these groups help friendship to grow, because they provide ways for people to be together and do things together.

Martin Luther King, Jr., and Ralph Abernathy, two young Southern black ministers, met in Montgomery, Alabama, in 1954. In the years that followed they did many things together—working, preaching, lobbying, marching in protest, sitting in protest, writing letters, comforting the oppressed.

ᴇ❦ *"The gift reveals the giver's heart"*

"Ralph became my husband's best friend," wrote Coretta King. Their friendship was rooted in doing things together to bring about racial equality.

Even the obituary that King wrote for himself defined him as a friend who did things. It said,

> Tell them I tried to feed the hungry.
> Tell them I tried to clothe the naked.
> Tell them I tried to help somebody.[6]

People don't have to belong to organizations to become friends or to do things together. Moreover, the things friends do together need not be serious or earth-shaking. Friends may enjoy sharing a bicycle ride, telling funny stories to each other, spending a night out at the theater, or working side by side on a project or hobby.

Anthropologist Louis Leakey, who made important discoveries of prehistoric humans in Africa, developed his close friendship with Donald MacInnes when he saw how skilled MacInnes was at reassembling prehistoric skull bones. Doing things together was an important part of their friendship.

Some people have a number of friends and do different things with each of them. John, a psychotherapist, and Howard, a cost analyst, were involved in running a group home for rejected children. Often they spent Saturdays making repairs in the home. Howard knew how to solve electrical problems. John had other third selves. One was with Norma, his wife. Based on the shared experience of keeping house and raising a family, they found many things to do together at home and ideas to talk about.

John had other third selves. One was with Norma, his wife, based on the shared experience of keeping house and raising a family. They found many things to do together at home and ideas to talk about.

---

6. Coretta Scott King, *My Life with Martin Luther King, Jr.* (New York: Holt, Rinehart & Winston, 1969; Avon ed.), pp. 117, 335.

    "Let's do something together"

Another of John's third selves was with Gail, a married woman on his staff. They enjoyed working together with teen-agers who needed counseling, and caring for the plants they purchased jointly for the office. They also enjoyed friendship with each other's spouses in another third self made up of *four people,* John and his wife plus Gail and her husband. The two couples often vacationed together, going in one car and sharing the same cottage. Doing things together was at the basis of their relationship.

Care and Concern

Caring is a third expectancy, and among friends it means helping the other grow. It appears in the welcome, warmth and nurturing activities friends do for each other.

Milton Mayeroff suggests that caring implies concern for a third self. He writes:

> In caring as helping the other grow, I experience what I care for (a person, an ideal, an idea) as an extension of myself and at the same time as something separate from me that I respect in its own right.[7]

Caring is not the same as using the other person to satisfy one's own needs. Neither is it to be confused with such things as well-wishing, or simply having an interest in what happens to another. Caring is a process of helping others grow and actualize themselves. It is a transforming experience.

Care and concern are expected between friends, especially in times of crisis. Gentle feminist author and poet Anaïs Nin had friends who often sought her care and concern. Many of them were famous authors and writers. One was Edmund Wilson, whom colleagues described as unimaginative, unemotional and purely intellectual. Among certain of his friends this seemingly cold and aloof man allowed his feelings to pour out.

On a cold and damp January day in England, near the end of the Second World War, Anaïs Nin wrote in her diary,

---

7. Milton Mayeroff, *On Caring* (New York: Harper & Row, 1971), p. 5.

Edmund Wilson invited me for lunch. I felt his distress, received his confession. Even though not an intimate friend, Wilson senses my sympathy and turns toward it. He is lonely and lost. He is going to France as a war correspondent. He asks me to accompany him as he buys his uniform, his sleeping bag. We talk. He tells me about his suffering with Mary McCarthy.[8]

When things get rough, friends are likely to look to each other for nurturing. When self-esteem is low, they look for encouragement. When emotions are frayed, friends need lifting up.

Difficult times often test the strength of a third self. According to Albert Schweitzer,

Sometimes our light goes out but it is blown again into flame by an encounter with another human being. Each of us owes the deepest thanks to those who have rekindled this inner light.

Many traditionally personal expressions of care and concern have been taken over by *institutions*, such as state or federal government, insurance companies, unions or business corporations.

Family or friends used to care for others who were sick. Now people are expected to have health insurance, or, in the case of the elderly, to turn to Medicare. In time of retirement, family or friends used to extend care. Now retired people fall back on corporate retirement plans and social security.

Yet, friends still show many examples of caring for each other. For example, friends still help each other move. They bring food to a sick friend, and drive a friend's children, or a number of friends' children, in a car pool. They volunteer to help friends in a project, or babysit for their children.

Joe brought his wife Lenor back to his small hometown of

8. *The Diary of Anaïs Nin, Volume Four, 1944–1947* (New York: Harcourt, Brace, Jovanovich, 1971), p. 41. Mary McCarthy was his wife at the time.

Tracy, California, where they had a three-hundred-acre farm. Joe's friends and neighbors were mainly farmers.

Just before planting time, Lenor had to have her leg amputated. Joe took her to Mayo Clinic in Minnesota, where they stayed for almost a month. Happy as they were with her good recovery, the young couple were discouraged because as they rode home they had lost their chance for a crop that year.

Their sadness turned to smiles when they arrived home. Friends and neighbors had not only been "praying for Lenor," but the whole town of Tracy had turned out to plow and plant their three hundred acres. For good measure, the town had also landscaped their front yard.

Joe and Lenor had friends who cared.

Honesty among Friends

Honesty among friends is an almost universal expectancy. Robert Louis Stevenson claimed, "We are all travelers in this world, and the best companion we can find in our travels is an honest friend." Third-self friendship cannot live with deception or dishonesty.

Honesty in friendship does not mean friends must tell each other *everything*, as teen-agers often do.

In symbiotic relationships, where the friends feel there is really only "one self" (Viewpoint 1), partners usually feel that to be honest they must tell each other everything. But honesty need not contradict personal privacy. Friends, if they choose, are entitled to keep their personal lives to themselves and to maintain privacy about other friendships.

Cynthia Marshall Rich related a story of a child's need for privacy.

> When I was a little girl I wrote something on a piece of paper, something that didn't matter much, but it mattered to me because it was a private thought. My father came into my room and saw me shove the paper under the blotter, and he wanted

me to show it to him. So I quickly said, "No, it's private, I wrote it to myself, I didn't write it to be seen," but he said he wanted to see it. And I said, "No, no, no, it was silly anyway," and he said, "Sarah Ann, nothing you have to say would seem silly to me, you never give me credit for understanding, I can understand a great deal," but I said it wasn't just him, really it wasn't, because I hadn't written it for anyone at all to see. Then he was all sad and hurt and said this wasn't a family where we keep things hidden and there I was hiding this from him. I heard his voice, and it went on and on, and he said I had no faith in him and that I shouldn't keep things from him—and I said it wasn't anything big or special, it was just some silly nonsense, but if it was nonsense, he said, why wouldn't I let him read it, since it would make him happy? And I cried and cried, because it was only a very little piece of paper and why did he have to see it anyway, but he was very solemn and said if you held back little things soon you would be holding back bigger things and the gap would grow wider and wider. So I gave him the paper. He read it and said nothing except that I was a good girl and he couldn't see what all the fuss had been about.[9]

Privacy is a privilege of any self. Since close friendships usually involve three selves—you, me, and our third self—there are three selves to enjoy the privilege.

Honesty among friends involves the mutual sharing of expectations and assumptions *concerning their third self.* Honest friendship can create a climate that allows people to tell each other, as they never have before, what's really going on inside them.

On the other hand, what one hopes to find in the relationship may not be what the other expects. "If I assume," said one friend to another, "that we will see each other at least once every week, and you assume that it will be okay to meet merely once a month, misunderstandings may arise."

Honesty asks friends to express themselves clearly from time to time and to resolve whatever conflicts may arise before they interfere with the health of the third self. Friends

9. Cynthia Marshall Rich, "My Sister's Marriage," *Mademoiselle*, 1955.

strengthened by honesty feel comfortable and safe with each other.

Confidentiality and Loyalty

Confidentiality is often defined as keeping another's secret. It is part of what some people describe as trust. Friendship can hardly develop without it.

When friends share confidences, they expect their partners to be discreet and not to reveal publicly what they have heard as private information. Some friends clearly spell out the limits of confidentiality. Others simply assume it. Those involved in a third self of friendship always know that it exists and that it can be counted on.

In one way, the film, *The Lady Sings the Blues*, was about a lack of trust. It told the sad story of sensitive and volatile jazz vocalist Billie Holiday, who ended up trusting nobody—and for good reason.

Gentle Billie suffered continual and merciless humiliation as a black woman traveling with white musicians during the prejudice-ridden years of the thirties and forties.

Black singer Lena Horne, who knew Billie well, wrote of her:

> Her life was so tragic and so corrupted by other people—by white people and by her own people. There was no place for her to go, except, finally, into that little private world of dope. She was just too sensitive to survive. And such a gentle person. We never talked much about singing. The thing I remember talking to her about most was her dogs; her animals were really her only trusted friends.[10]

Her dogs were the only ones who had not betrayed Billie's confidentiality, and, without trust, she was unable to form third-self friendships with people.

10. Lena Horne with Richard Schickel, *Lena* (Garden City, N.Y.: Doubleday, 1965).

While confidentiality focuses on words, *loyalty* is likely to be expressed in actions.

Loyalty sometimes involves fighting for a friend, standing up for one when things are tough. Walter Winchell once defined a friend in terms of loyalty. "A friend," he said, "is one who walks in when others walk out."

Understanding and Empathy

Understanding and *empathy* are bonuses on the list of expectancies in most friendships. A third-self friendship that enjoys understanding and empathy is usually a strong one.

Generally, understanding has to do with knowing, empathy with feeling. Among friends, understanding involves getting into each other's minds; empathy, into each other's feelings.

Understanding requires clear communication. It requires one friend's willingness to express needs, feelings, and wishes as accurately as possible, and the second friend's active listening.

"It is certain," writes John Powell, "that a relationship will only be as good as its communication."

Therapist Virginia Satir, developer of conjoint family therapy and author of a penetrating book on communication called *Peoplemaking*, asserts,

> Once a human being has arrived on this earth, communication is the largest single factor determining what kinds of relationships he makes with others and what happens to him in the world about him.[11]

Empathy implies the ability to enter into another's feelings. Frequently, people feel an emotion intensely and *assume* that their friend perceives, feels and understands it. But that isn't always the case; the friend's thoughts and feelings may be somewhere else. It is unrealistic to expect friends to understand one's feelings intuitively.

11. Virginia Satir, *Peoplemaking* (Palo Alto, Calif.: Science and Behavior Books, 1972), p. 30.

Mutual understanding of feelings and ideas grows if communication is open. This may be one reason why presidential wife Betty Ford appointed Nancy Lee Howe as her special assistant. Betty and Nancy had been telephone friends for about a year before Gerald Ford became President.

"Nowadays," wrote a reporter, "Nancy Howe is the first person Betty Ford calls for when she gets up in the morning —about nine o'clock. By that time, Nancy has arrived at the White House and has thought through the First Lady's commitments and schedule for the day." [12]

Nancy's job involves being a sister, a personal shopper, a confidante and a spirit uplifter. The two women enjoy an uncommon understanding and empathy.

Betty owes her very life to Nancy, who insisted the First Lady have a breast cancer test. In empathy, Nancy would have gone even further. "I wish it could have been me who endured the operation for her."

Priorities in Friendship

Many people belong to several close or third-self friendships.

Knowingly or unknowingly, they rank their friendships in an order of importance to them. They may say, "Harry is my best friend, and Charles is second best" or "Cheryl is more special to me than Lisa."

At any one time, people may also have friends on a special need list. This may change their priorities, at least temporarily. They may say, "Mitch needs me tonight because he's all alone" or "Sara comes first this time because she will be leaving tomorrow for the whole summer."

Priorities in friendship often shift back and forth. At a certain time in a person's life one specific "we" may take priority over other "we's." When Linda's friend Sally was grieving

12. Frances Spatz Leighton, "New Job at the White House: Betty Ford's Best Friend," *Family Weekly*, March 2, 1975, p. 6.

over her father's death, Sally was "first" on Linda's *priority* list during that grief period although Sally is not usually ranked highest in *importance* among Linda's friends. When a crisis runs its course, another "we" may become the focus of attention or time or energy.

In the face of good news, one friend may *expect* the other to change priorities, for example, to stop working and join in a celebration. "Ginny is getting married on Saturday. I know it's short notice, but could you drive in from Chicago for the wedding?"

In the face of bad news, one may expect the other to stop working and join in the tears. "Lance, I do hope you can let the research project rest for a few days and fly home for Uncle Ed's funeral."

At other times, some people may feel *compelled* to act optimistic to please a happy friend, instead of crying for hours about some personal bad news.

Conflict may arise if the friends have different priorities, and are unwilling to change priorities for the occasion, celebrating or mourning, as the case may be.

Misunderstanding between friends about priorities may threaten the friendship. To maintain mutual understanding and empathy, third-self friends sometimes need to discuss and work through problems of priorities.

"One should keep his friendships in constant repair," cautioned Samuel Johnson.

❧ 6 ❧

The Needs of Friendship

"I need all the friends I can get."
CHARLIE BROWN, *Peanuts*

The need for friendship is as deep as the need for food or sleep. In fact, friendship is closely connected with all human needs.

According to psychologist Abraham Maslow, "Basic human needs can be fulfilled *only* by and through other human beings." [1]

Singer Carole King made famous a song called, "You've Got a Friend." The song's basic message was that friends help each other in times of need, "when you're down and troubled and you need some loving care." [2]

People like to know that they can call someone when they are in need, that somewhere there is someone who cares.

Carole's song asks, "Ain't it good to know that you've got a friend?" And everyone replies, "Yes."

Someone Who Cared

Mrs. Torres, a seventy-three-year-old widow, lived in a lower-

1. Abraham Maslow, *Religion, Values and Peak Experiences* (New York: Viking), preface to 1970 edition, p. xiii.
2. Carole King, "You've Got a Friend," copyright © 1971, Screen Gems-Columbia Music, Inc., New York.

income housing project in a depressed part of San Francisco. Meager government checks came regularly on the first of each month, yet by the 25th her face often looked more tired than usual and her eyes conveyed despairing hunger. It was hard to pinch pennies every day and she sometimes forgot how long a month could be.

Months would start out well. Mrs. Torres would take the bus across town to Golden Gate Park to visit the museum and the Japanese Tea Garden. Good feelings at the tea garden often influenced her to enjoy tea and cookies twice on the same day, though it upset her budget.

One night she was accosted by a purse snatcher. With what seemed to be superhuman strength, she kicked the young thief. He grabbed for his ankle and let go of her purse strap; she stumbled through the door of the apartment house, shaking with fear. Mr. Ballard, a seventy-one-year-old man who also lived alone, had seen the episode from his third-floor window, and rushed down to help. He stood at the doorway yelling and shaking his fist in the direction of the vanishing hoodlum.

When Mr. Ballard helped her to her room, he couldn't help noticing Mrs. Torres's empty food shelves and the next-to-last teabag that she shared with him. Sitting across the table with someone who seemed to care, the woman poured out her anxiety about money. Though normally stoic and uncomplaining, Mrs. Torres cried.

Mr. Ballard patted her hand. Luckily, he explained, he got his check on the 24th of each month. When her money ran out she could come to his place, use his food, and cook for them both. At first Mrs. Torres refused. "What would others think!" Finally, when he agreed to cook for her when *his* money ran out, she agreed.

The friendship between Mrs. Torres and Mr. Ballard started with their common concern for food and safety. People willing to share what they have and shake their fists at a common enemy may provide each other with a feeling of basic security.

Food and safety are important human needs. A matrix in which needs are met may contribute to the development of a third self.

A Deeper Affinity

Friends who call out to each other in need may share a deeper affinity than they suspect. There *may* be an interesting relationship between friendship and blood chemistry.

In a 1935 Canadian medical journal, a social worker reported that when he had "difficult children" to place in foster homes, he sometimes did blood typing. Problems seldom arose when he placed a "difficult child" with a family whose children had the same blood type as the foster child's. In fact, the children often became friends.

A rural Canadian doctor, Hugh Campbell Brown, told the following story to one of the authors. One day, during his first year of medical practice forty years ago in a small isolated town, he had to give a blood transfusion. The town had no serum for blood typing, and no blood transfusion services, so he faced the laborious task of cross matching sera and cells of prospective donors with the patient's.

"I remembered reading an article on cross matching," said the doctor, "and asked the patient who his closest friend was. He named someone I had already tested but who hadn't matched. So I asked again, 'Is this really your closest friend?' "

"He said, 'Well, he's my brother-in-law, and I see a lot of him but if I have real problems, I go up to an old Swede trapper in the hills and have a bull session.'

"I sent the police to find the Swedish trapper; and, on cross matching, I found they did match."

Whether chemical attraction is due to some basic affinity and contributes to close and third-self friendships remains a tentative and intriguing hypothesis until more research is done.

In various cultures throughout history friends have cut themselves and mingled their blood in symbolic acts of oneness. Could there be some other reason?

Hierarchy of Needs

According to psychologist Abraham Maslow, everyone has a hierarchy of needs which are determining factors in their lives, though people may not be fully aware of them. Needs often move people, sometimes unknowingly, into relationships in which the needs can be met.

Clarifying needs is one way to understand some processes and expectancies of friendship. People may be attracted to each other because in some way they hope (expect) the relationship will meet their needs. Maslow diagrams human needs on a pyramid: Basic needs form a strong foundation, growth needs rest on top.

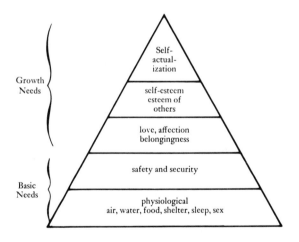

Basic Needs

Everyone has the basic needs essential for bodily survival which are located at the base of Maslow's pyramid. They include the *physiological needs:* for air, water, food, shelter, sleep and sexual expression. Everyone also has basic needs for *safety* and *security*.

All basic needs affect motivation and behavior. People who are usually hungry, thirsty, cold and tired have great difficulty forming relationships that enhance their human growth. For most people, unless basic needs are met, growth needs cannot be, but once basic needs are met, friendship may develop around one or more of the growth needs.

Adults whose basic needs are all cared for may become preoccupied with their own growth needs. A group of middle-class teachers started a summer camp program for impoverished children.

> Our idea was to share with these deprived children some of the "higher things in life" that we knew. But at camp the children didn't respond. Arts and craft boxes were left untouched. The kids only reluctantly participated in friendship games. And they consistently refused to be artistically creative.

> Instead, their primary interests seemed to be eating, fighting with each other, and feeling safe. Kids from the same neighborhoods stayed together and were suspicious of other children. They found ways to lock and barricade their cabins at night, "for protection from enemies." And they seemed afraid of the forest and asked many questions about how dangerous it was.

Puzzled at the children's lack of response to their program, the teachers turned to a psychologist. He showed them Maslow's need pyramid. After a moment's reflection, the teachers recognized that they had presumed that the children at camp were operating near the top of the pyramid. Instead, the children, coming from near-poverty families in inner-city apartments, focused their attention on more basic matters near the bottom. They were naturally concerned about physiological, safety and security needs, since the forest camp was for them a strange environment with unfamiliar people.

Physiological Needs

People live in their bodies. This simple statement has impli-

⇛ *"People live in their bodies"*

cations that are sometimes neglected. Bodies need air, sleep, water and food if they are to stay alive.

Few people know that Ed Sullivan cared for the basic needs of his old friend Johnny Dundee. Until he died, the almost penniless ex-prize-fighter received a weekly check from the television celebrity to cover his needs.[3]

People whose basic needs are satisfied only at a minimal level are often impoverished emotionally or intellectually. The sheer struggle for existence may be so all-consuming that such people have little energy left for any kind of friendships.

This struggle for survival was often necessary among people who worked long hours at hard physical labor, in places like farm fields, coal mines and factories before wage-and-hour laws were common, or among those who kept house, tended babies, cooked and cleaned, especially before the days of modern conveniences.

In such cases, fatigue and exhaustion depleted the physical resources necessary for developing close relationships. There was seldom enough time or energy to pursue third-self friendships.

One of the mysteries of the third self is that, although it is without its own body, it requires bodies of friends if it is to come into existence. Once a friendship is born, however, its *memory* may sustain it beyond space, time, bodies, and even death.

Medical problems may also inhibit development of a third self. People afflicted with functional glycemia are likely to experience frequent depression and confusion. These feelings may be so overpowering that such people find no motivation to form friendships.

Similarly, the physically handicapped or those suffering from inconvenient, painful or terminal illness may feel prohibited from friendship. As one young man with cerebral palsy

3. Michael David Harris, *Always on Sunday: Ed Sullivan, An Inside View* (New York: Meredith Press, 1968), p. 18.

expressed it, "I feel as if I am alone on an island, unable to make contact with the rest of the human mainland."

Happily, there are people who, though physically ill, impoverished, or handicapped, are nevertheless able to form friendships. Helen Keller, blind and unable to speak from birth, was one of these. Her adult life was full of friendships, thanks to the patience of her teacher, Anne Sullivan.

During the depression years, folksinger Jimmy Rodgers kept up a cheery manner although he was wasting away from tuberculosis. Instead of wailing for sympathy, he sang of the troubles of poor whites, communicating to them the understanding of a friend. A biographer wrote:

> When his audiences of railroad workers, truck drivers, laborers, farmers, and small-town people heard his songs, they recognized him as one of their own, and the deadening, bleak years of the depression were thereby made more endurable.[4]

Sexual Expression

Another bodily need is sexual expression. While people can live without this need being directly filled, it continues to influence their behavior.

Knowingly or unknowingly, people may attract or repel potential friends with sexual signs. Perfume and shaving lotion are common come-ons, and what one person likes, another may avoid. People may almost smell out new friends—either with or without awareness.

Friendship may follow or precede an erotic attraction. However, erotic attraction may exist without friendship and friendship without erotic attraction.

The many people "who bury" or deny their sexual feelings have little awareness of the power of their sexual needs. Nevertheless, repressed sexual feelings may suddenly come

4. Henry Pleasants, *The Great American Popular Singers* (New York: Simon & Schuster, 1974).

into conscious awareness indirectly expressed in feelings of resentment or anger. This happens because sexual feelings are associated with fear, guilt or anxiety. Sexual feelings may also be sublimated into "higher" emotions, such as those connected with religion, art, nurturing and humanitarian pursuits.

Sarah Bernhardt's life was an example of the indirect expression of sexual feelings. Biographers described the world-famous actress as "above all a great and tempestuous lover." However, in her teen years, Sarah suppressed her feelings of sexual attraction toward men.

> In my teens I cared nothing for men—they disgusted me. I was called a great beauty and men used to kneel at my feet and swear that they would jump in the Seine if I refused them. Invariably I told them to go and do so! I was indifferent to all men.[5]

Instead the young Sarah redirected her emotional energy.

First, she wished to be a nun. "I would like to die with my soul dedicated to God," she said. Next, it was a passion for the theater; she found herself staying for performance after performance at the Opera Comique. She explored her budding artistic talents and won a first prize for her painting, "Winter in the Champs Elysées." After that it was sculpture. All these interests surfaced during her teen years. Only later in her life was she able to accept herself as the sexually passionate woman she was.

When physical need is directly expressed, it may be with words, actions or both. Words may range from passionate statements to subtle innuendoes. Actions may be as light as a brief touch or glance, or as intense as sexual intercourse. Sexual needs may or may not be part of a close or a third-self friendship.

---

5. Basil Woon, *The Real Sarah Bernhardt: As Told to Her Friend Mme. Pierre Berton* (New York: Liveright Publishing Corp., 1924), p. 63.

Safety Needs

Another mystery of the third self is the need for physical and emotional safety and, by extension, security and protection. If one member of a third self moves to a distant place, becomes seriously ill or dies, the sense of safety experienced in the relationship may be seriously threatened.

Joan, a young married woman who had enjoyed a deep friendship with a neighbor, said in a group-therapy session: "I can't stand it. I feel so vulnerable now that Ramona has moved so far away. I could always count on her when things would go wrong. Like when I fell off a ladder and broke my leg and couldn't move, and I hollered and she came. Or, like once when the kids were so sick and we were scared half to death."

"I know what you mean," chimed in Michael. "When I was in college I had a friend that I could count on when things got tough. We'd lend each other five bucks, help each other cram for finals, and all that. Somehow, I felt so *safe* knowing Tom. He was always there, and I could count on him."

The fact that some people feel fearful at the depth of their beings indicates that the basic need for safety remains unsatisfied in them. They may have been temporarily or permanently abandoned in childhood, physically and emotionally brutalized, or verbally threatened or ridiculed in some way that left them feeling raw, exposed, unprotected and unsafe. Since the basic safety needs were not met, their fear carries over into later life.

Even without an unhappy childhood, fear may be experienced in later life.

A person faced with unemployment or impaired by injury or illness will usually feel unsafe. The death of a spouse after years of a mutually protective marriage sometimes arouses fear in the survivor. A pending divorce may be frightening to a person who is not self-supporting, or who has grown accustomed to having his or her physical and emotional needs met exclusively by the other.

A paralyzing emotion, fear accompanies any threat to a person's safety. Friendship softens the threat. Comrades who have developed a close or third-self friendship can face an enemy with more equilibrium than if they are alone.

Eldridge Cleaver had been serving time in California for nearly nine years. "I'm perfectly aware that I'm in prison," he wrote from Folsom Prison, "that I'm a Negro, that I've been a rapist, and that I have a Higher Uneducation." He was a thirty-one-year-old "soul on ice."

Beverly Axelrod was a San Francisco lawyer. On impulse, Mr. Cleaver wrote to her asking for legal assistance. She came, tossed him a lifeline, became his lawyer and his friend.

Later, he wrote to her recalling the night of his first letter to her.

> If only you knew how I'd been drowning, how I'd considered that I'd gone down for the third time long ago, how I kept thrashing around in the water simply because I still felt the impulse to fight back and the tug of the distant shore, how I sat in a rage that night with the polysyllabic burden of your name pounding in my brain—Beverly Axelrod, Beverly Axelrod—and out of what instinct did I decide to write to you? It was a gamble on an equation constructed in delirium, and it was right.[6]

Friends respond in crisis. It is not unusual for victims of flood, famine, pestilence, or fire to struggle for life if, at the edge of death, they are called back to life by the other part of their third self.

Many people share extrasensory experiences of telepathy and clairvoyance, and those who are emotionally close may experience feelings of potential danger if the safety of a friend is threatened. One may call out mentally to the other in

6. Eldridge Cleaver, *Soul on Ice* (New York: Dell Publishing Co., 1968), pp. 18, 143.

anguish and terror, and the voice be "heard" hundreds of miles away perhaps because of the phenomenon of the third self. "You came just when I needed you to help me bear the pain," said Vicki to her friend.

Love and Belongingness

Everyone needs love and belongingness. This is one reason people join groups, teams, and associations. A desire for companionship is a major factor motivating people to work together, play together, and live together.

Belongingness is a major reason for people getting married and establishing families. According to a University of Michigan survey, wives were asked to select what they liked best in marriage. "Companionship" ranked first in a list of five items.

1st place —companionship
2nd place—a chance to have children
3rd place —husband's understanding of wife's problems and feelings
4th place —husband's expressions of love and affection
5th place —material things (a certain standard of living)

People may marry out of love, but a large part of the permanent emotional nourishment in marriage comes from companionship. It is a quality closely related to the growth need of belongingness.

The need to belong is felt early in life. Children naturally want to belong to a family. It is also common for them to get together, form clubs and build treehouses for secret meetings with others belonging to their inner circle.

For young adults, belongingness needs are expressed when they join swimming teams, sororities and fraternities, choirs, marching bands and cycling clubs. Dating and having "steady" boyfriends or girlfriends also satisfy belonging needs during adolescence.

Throughout life, Maslow says, "Love hunger is a deficiency disease like salt hunger or avitaminosis." Without proper nu-

❧ *"Everyone needs love and belongingness"*

trition, we are handicapped in some way, feel less strong and less able to cope. So it is without love and a sense of belonging. One of the highest suicide rates in the United States is among early middle-aged men who live alone, out of contact with friends or family.

When the sense of belongingness is missing or is threatened, people may begin to feel out of place, unwelcome. Their bodies then experience tension, fatigue or illness.

Families may break up because friendship that holds a family together is missing.[7] Whenever belongingness breaks down, a group's unity is threatened. As long as a sense of love and caring is alive in a group, individuals are able to fulfill their needs for giving and receiving affection.

The need for belongingness sometimes drives people into symbiotic ($\frac{1}{2} + \frac{1}{2} \rightarrow 1$) dependent relationships or keeps them in jobs that are boring and nonproductive. Many people stay in destructive marriages because they are afraid to take responsibility for living alone.

Belongingness and Loneliness

Three out of four divorced people remarry within five years —a high rate considering the pains that marriage must have brought them.

Why do they try again? Studies show that less than 5 percent of divorced people remarry for economic reasons. Sex, infatuation or need of a father (or mother) for the children are reasons lowest on the list. The dominant reason is companionship, "to be someone's friend and have a friend."

People remarry primarily because they are *lonely*.

Dag Hammarskjöld once wrote, "What makes loneliness an anguish is not that I have no one to share my burden, but this: I have only my own burden to bear." In other words,

7. See Muriel James, *TA for Moms and Dads, op. cit.*, on Maslow's needs reflected in the family and how parents can function to meet their own and their children's needs.

the pain of loneliness is strongest when one realizes that there is no "ourself" (third self).

People are often willing to put up with physical and emotional agony, and to change their lifestyles in the hope of belonging. They will learn to dance and play chess. They will change jobs, move to unpleasant places, work, fight and struggle for potential "we's" and the dream of a third self.

In a family, if one person seeks friendship with another family member and is rejected, the pain can be intense.

Suzanne had many friends. Mary, her twenty-five-year-old handicapped daughter, had few. "Please," Suzanne begged her sister, Ann, "Please phone your niece, or drop her a card, or even ask her over. Please, do it once a year or so. Mary needs to feel that she belongs to our family." Suzanne's sister was too busy. So was her brother. Only a neighborhood friend, understood the anguish and responded.

Suzanne knew the importance of the feeling of belongingness in her daughter's life.

Esteem Needs

The need for esteem—self-esteem and esteem from other people—is the next growth need that Maslow sees as important.

People who esteem themselves feel competent, confident, accepting and independent. They are able to accomplish more than people who have feelings of inferiority and inadequacy, and to do so without a sense of compulsion or competition. Esteemed by others, they feel the respect and appreciation and tend to become even more competent.

Television's Ed Sullivan and his wife, Sylvia, had a mutual self-esteem society. When Sylvia would leave the table at a nightclub, Ed was likely to watch her walking away and mutter under his breath, "She sure is a terrific girl." Sylvia, in turn, did her part to keep Ed's esteem high. He once recalled:

> Sylvia is a great rooting section for me. More than once she has believed in me enough to stand behind me on a gamble.

. . . If it hadn't been for her, I'm sure I wouldn't be where I am now. She has always been the silent and powerful chorus in the background. Hers has been the grim and lonely job of waiting and watching; no matter what I've done, she's been there.[8]

Friendships between self-esteeming people frequently focus on mutual respect for each other's achievements.

Friends Karen and Marlene worked in the same beauty shop. Both were creative hair stylists who delighted when the other solved a difficult hair problem. They frequently attended classes to up-date their skills, and vacationed together at the beach. Lying in the sun, they would spend long hours talking about the meaning of life.

World-famous Los Angeles Dodgers' pitcher Sandy Koufax recalled the bonds of belongingness and esteem baseball teammates experience.

"For as long as I can remember, I have been playing sports," he said, "and for as long as I can remember, my best friends have been my teammates. The camaraderie of the locker room is one of the greatest pleasures."

The need for esteem—a sense of success—is also met mutually by teammates.

There is among us all a far closer relationship than the purely social one of a fraternal organization because we are bound together not only by a single interest but by a common goal: to win! Nothing else matters and nothing else will do.[9]

Self-esteeming people plan their lives so that they are able to be independent. Freedom is important to them. They feel confident in their abilities to learn new things, find ways to solve new problems, make thoughtful and autonomous decisions. Because they are esteemed by others, they often receive

8. Michael David Harris, *Always on Sunday: Ed Sullivan, An Inside View*, pp. 60–61.
9. Sandy Koufax with Ed Linn, *Koufax* (New York: Viking, 1966), pp. 6–7.

recognition, acceptance and appreciation. Their reputations include being trustworthy.

Maslow claims, "The most stable and, therefore, the most healthy self-esteem is based on *deserved* respect from others rather than on external fame or celebrity and unwarranted adulation." [10]

Because he was insecure as a person, Al Jolson continually needed his self-esteem boosted. "He needed applause the way a diabetic needs insulin," wrote Pearl Sieben in *The Immortal Jolson*. In him, something went wrong with the need mechanism. Even the unprecedented success Jolson received "as the greatest entertainer the world has ever known" did not satisfy his need for esteem.

Jolson's insecurity prevented him from freely forming deep friendships. Even the all-loving Eddie Cantor referred to Jolson only as a "neighbor."

> We walked together, talked together, ate together, and I knew him better than I had ever known him through the years. What amazed me was that this great personality had never learned how to live. He couldn't; there was something chemically wrong. The minute the curtain rang down, he died.[11]

Self-Actualizing Needs

The self-actualizing needs at the top of Maslow's pyramid include growth in: truth, goodness, beauty, aliveness, individuality, perfection, justice, order, simplicity, playfulness and self-sufficiency.

Persons living at this uppermost growth level have met their basic, belonging and esteem needs. They tend to be "spontaneous, expressive, natural and free—almost as if they had

10. Abraham H. Maslow, *Motivation and Personality* (New York: Harper & Row, 1954).
11. Eddie Cantor with Jane Kesner Ardmore, *Take My Life* (Garden City, N.Y.: Doubleday, 1957).

got to the top of the hill and were now coasting down the other side." [12]

Few people realize that world-renowned scientist Albert Einstein dedicated forty years of his life to abolishing war. His writings on peace fill a book of over seven hundred tightly printed pages. A few days before his death he affixed the last signature of his life to a statement drafted by close friend Bertrand Russell urging the abolition of war.

The self-actualizing needs of peace, justice and truth remained continually before Einstein. They formed a bond between him and his friends. He once said,

> In matters concerning truth and justice there can be no distinction between big problems and small; for the general principles which determine the conduct of men are indivisible. Whoever is careless with the truth in small matters cannot be trusted in important affairs.[13]

Friendships between self-actualizing people often develop out of similar concern for things such as justice and beauty. With mutual enjoyment, some people share their joys and jokes while discovering the essential third self that can exist between them.

Probably everyone has occasionally experienced peak experience *moments* when they were "hitting on all cylinders." A peak experience is a taste of self-actualization. Self-actualizing friends seem to enjoy such moments more often than others.

Friendships between people who allow themselves to grow, and are not afraid to develop their growth-need potentials, add to the self-actualization of each person. Peak moments occur in their relationships in which beauty, truth and wholeness are experienced.

Research genius George Washington Carver developed a deep

---

12. Frank Goble, *The Third Force* (New York: Grossman Publishers, 1970), p. 46.
13. *Einstein on Peace,* ed. by Otto Nathan and Heinz Norden (New York: Schocken Books, 1960), p. 639.

"conversational" friendship with God. Colleagues sometimes wondered if the black agricultural chemist was a religious fanatic or a profound philosopher. His scientific contributions could not be denied: salad oil, an oil remedy for infantile paralysis, stains and face powder from clays, flour and shoe polish from sweet potatoes, paving blocks from cotton, dyes from dandelions, peanuts, tomato vines and trees.

Carver claimed his source of knowledge and genius was his friend God, or "Dear Mr. Creator."

> I have made it a rule to get up every morning at four. I go into the woods and there I gather specimens and study the great lessons that Nature is eager to teach us. Alone in the woods each morning I best hear and understand God's plan for me. . . . I'll only listen to his voice and try to carry out his instructions.[14]

Carver refused to take money for his services. His monthly salary checks from Tuskegee Institute often lay in the financial office safe for ten years before he claimed them. All he wanted was a place to work—to dream and plan ways to improve the earth, to make it a better place for people to live.

In the present century, many groups around the world continue to gather in friendship to seek higher values such as peace, equality and human rights.

Martin Luther King, Jr., and his friends initiated new directions in the civil rights movement. They worked to fill the need for equality and unity among socially deprived people.

From all over the world people come to Israel to experience the friendship and unity of the *kibbutzim*. Speaking of these cooperative settlements, Israel's then prime minister David Ben-Gurion said, "I believe we are capable of being a light for other nations. We are not better than other people, but we certainly do things that other people do not do." [15]

14. Shirley Graham and George D. Lipscomb, *Dr. George Washington Carver, Scientist* (New York: Julian Messner, 1944).
15. Robert St. John, *Ben-Gurion: A Biography* (Garden City, N.Y.: Doubleday, 1971), p. 351.

Millions of women throughout the world are joining movements for equal rights. Together they are creating opportunities for women to fulfill their higher needs.

Each year more and more people seeking transcendent experience visit the religious monasteries of the East. Many stay for months or years, and bring back to the West the wisdom they discovered in the atmosphere of quiet friendship among Hindu, Buddhist and Zen monks. Close and third-self friendships tend toward a common involvement in self-actualizing values. They encourage a striving to transform the world and promote human unity. At the same time, they urge friends to act creatively toward each other.

The history of civilization presents a continuous waterfall of some friendships built upon higher concerns.

The Pull of Beauty

Beauty is another self-actualizing need mentioned by Maslow. Friends who are artists know the deep inner pull of beauty.

Chaim Potok tells the story of Asher Lev, a sixteen-year-old oil-painting prodigy who came from an orthodox Jewish family in Brooklyn. A famous Jewish sculptor, Jacob Kahn, about sixty years older than Asher, became first his teacher, then his friend. A Hasidic Jew, Asher was torn between his religious beliefs, which were deep and genuine needs to him, and his vocation to art.

One summer Asher went to live and work with Kahn in a house on the edge of a Cape Cod sand dune. He recalled,

> Often in the early mornings, I came out of the house and walked across the dunes to the beach. The dunes were cool then from the night. . . . those mornings, the beach was my synagogue and the waves and gulls were audience to my prayers. I stood on the beach and felt wind-blown sprays of ocean on my face, and I prayed.[16]

16. Chaim Potok, *My Name Is Asher Lev* (New York: Knopf, 1972), p. 252.

The old sculptor taught Asher how to fulfill his need for beauty without losing his need to relate to God.

"I talk to God through my sculpture and painting," said Kahn simply.

Together in friendship, dedicated to their belief in God and their love of beauty, they helped bring out the deepest potential in each other.

One day that summer, Asher told his friend, "I am going to be an artist."

Jacob Kahn replied unhesitatingly, "You have been an artist for a long time, Asher Lev."

Full Potential

Friendship calls for growth. It must be chosen over and over again. What people *can* be, they *must* be, claims Maslow. "This is the desire to become more and more of what one is, to become everything that one is capable of becoming."

Unfortunately, although every relationship has the capacity to grow into a self-actualizing third self, many do not realize their full potentials. If fear or anxiety enters a relationship, there is often a retreat to safety needs, security needs and old patterns of relating.

Change of Need Focus

Regardless of the matrix and the growth needs out of which a third self may develop, basic physical and safety needs may become overriding at any time. The new focus may be temporary or permanent, but when it happens, the friendship may change in some way.

A friendship built on mutual esteem for each other's artistic abilities can suddenly change and focus on safety during a natural catastrophe, such as flood or fire, when people respond to each other out of their common concern for safety. This might also happen when one friend loses a job or money, or experiences a divorce or the death of a family member.

One young couple spent years trying to make ends meet and to satisfy their own and their children's basic physical and safety needs. They noticed that when they were preoccupied with physical and safety needs, their feelings of love and belongingness were less intense. Gradually, the situation changed. After a few years in night school they were able to find better jobs, move to better housing, and pay their bills without agonizing. "Can you imagine," she said, "we've suddenly fallen in love again." "Yes, no wonder," he added, "I really respect what you've done with yourself and I feel good about me too."

Another example of change of focus involves two people with mutual esteem and appreciation on the job who may, with sudden or gradual awareness, experience a sexual attraction for each other. This is not uncommon; these needs—heterosexual or homosexual—may be felt by one or both persons, simply because sex is a basic human need.

In summary, the change from growth needs to basic needs or vice versa may occur at any time.

Sexual Attraction among Self-Actualizing Friends

Sexual attraction can produce stress in relationships where it is not expected or accepted, either enhancing the relationship or threatening it.

How to express sexual needs in a third self of friendship depends on how those involved define their third self and their expectancies for it.

Can people mix friendship and sex? Psychiatrist Theodore Reik believed that being a good friend and being a good sweetheart were mutually exclusive and contradictory. On the other hand, Abraham Maslow, working with self-actualizing people, found data that seem to indicate the contrary.

It is important to remember that Maslow is talking about sexual attraction among *self-actualizing friends*. In many ways, such friends are a "different breed." People do not usually make friends on the self-actualizing level unless all other human needs are being fulfilled in some way. Among self-actual-izing people, sexual *needs* are presumably being fulfilled in some way already. Therefore, if sexual feelings enter the relationship they probably spring from "choice" or "enjoy-ment," rather than from "need."

As a general principle, higher needs, like esteem and self-actualization, cannot usually be built until the lower ones, like physiological and safety needs, are cared for. But once these lower needs are satisfied, they recede from everyday aware-ness and there is little preoccupation with them.

An excellent parallel may be made between sensual enjoy-ment and the enjoyment of food. For people who have all the food they *need*, eating may be experienced on a different level, where foods may be "chosen" and "enjoyed." Maslow contends that self-actualizers' attitudes toward sex and eating are quite similar in certain ways.

> Food is simultaneously enjoyed and yet regarded as relatively unimportant in the total scheme of life by self-actualizing people. When they do enjoy it, they can enjoy it wholeheart-edly, and without the slightest tainting with bad attitudes toward animality and the like. And yet ordinarily, feeding oneself takes a relatively unimportant place in the total picture. These people do not *need* sensuality; they simply enjoy it when it occurs.[17]

According to Maslow, self-actualizers can wholeheartedly en-joy sex, sometimes far more than the average person. Yet at the same time sex does not play a central role in their total frame of reference. For them, the enjoyment of both sex and food pale in comparison to the need to work for justice, truth, beauty and world unity.[18]

On Many Levels

Those friendships are best that can satisfy needs on many

---

17. Abraham H. Maslow, *Motivation and Personality* (New York: Harper & Row, 1954), p. 243.
18. *Ibid.*

levels. If close or third-self relationships live at only one level of need, they are not likely to be as permanent as those that involve more levels. Self-actualizing people really "work" at involving many need levels in their relationship. They do this with self-discipline, creativity and flexibilty. For them, friends receive high priority since they give significant meaning to life.

❧ 7 ❧

The Transactions of Friendship

> We shall not cease from exploration
> and the end of all our exploring
> will be to arrive where we started
> and know the place for the first time.
> **T. S. ELIOT**

A True Friend

From the beginning of time, people have known the survival value of friendship and the tragedy if it is lost.

Francis Bacon said, "Without friends the world is but a wilderness."

The Roman poet Cicero wrote, "A true friend is more esteemed than kinfolk."

David Powers, close friend of John F. Kennedy, seemingly felt this way. He often left his family to be with Kennedy. Their relationship was an intimate one:

> Dave was accustomed to being summoned for night duty at the White House when Jackie was absent. He called himself "John's Other Wife." The President hated to be alone in the evening. It was understood that Dave would be available to keep him company in the mansion even on nights like this one, when Jackie would be out of the house for only a short time.
>
> During the summer months when Jackie and the children were at Hyannis Port and the President faced solitary confinement

 "*Without friends the world is but a wilderness*"

in Washington in the evenings from Monday until Thursday, Dave stayed with him until he went to bed. Their nightly routine was always the same. The White House kitchen staff would prepare a dinner of broiled chicken or lamb chops that would be left in the second floor apartment on a hot-plate appliance so that they could eat it late in the evening alone, without keeping any of the staff waiting to serve them. Then they would watch television, or sit outside on the Truman Balcony, or the President would read a book and smoke a cigar while Dave drank several bottles of his Heineken's beer. "All this Heineken's of mine that you're drinking costs me a lot of money, Dave," the President would say. "I'm going to send you a bill for it one of these days."

Around eleven o'clock, the President would get undressed and slip into the short-length Brooks Brothers sleeping jacket that he wore in preference to pajamas. Dave would watch him kneel beside his bed and say his prayers. Then he would get into bed, and say to Dave, "Goodnight, pal, will you please put out the light?" Dave would put out the light, leave the apartment, say goodnight again to the Secret Service agent on duty in the downstairs hall, and drive home to his own house in McLean, Virginia.[1]

Most people, including presidents, want parenting at times from their friends. The kind they want, such as putting out the light, may seem strange to others. The friendship between these two politicians began in 1946. Kennedy invited Powers to go to a meeting with him, even though Powers was campaigning for another candidate. Powers was so impressed with Kennedy's brief political address that he became a staunch supporter and close friend. When Kennedy was assassinated, November 22, 1963, Powers was riding in the car just behind him.

Many people in public office develop very close friendships with at least one other person. At times this other person acts in nurturing, protective ways. David Powers evidently did this for John F. Kennedy, Bebe Rebozo for Richard Nixon,

1. Kenneth O'Donnell and David F. Powers, "*Johnny, We Hardly Knew Ye*" (Boston: Little, Brown, 1972), p. 264.

Harry Hopkins for Franklin Roosevelt, and Sam Rayburn for Lyndon B. Johnson.

Transactional Analysis and Ego States

One of the most popular theories about people and how they relate to each other was developed by Eric Berne. It is called Transactional Analysis—TA for short.[2]

TA is based on the idea that everybody's personality has three parts, or ego states. These are called Parent, Adult, and Child. Each state is a unique system of feelings, attitudes and behaviors. Formed during childhood, they are carried throughout life.

For people, the Child ego state is the child they once were, the Parent ego state is made up of the parent figures who cared for them as children, and the Adult ego state refers to the data-gathering, rational, decision-making persons they sometimes are.

This is diagrammed as:

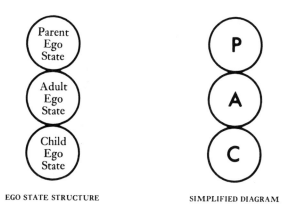

EGO STATE STRUCTURE   SIMPLIFIED DIAGRAM

2. TA was popularized in Eric Berne's book *Games People Play* (New York: Grove Press, 1967).

When activated, the Parent ego state may express care, concern or criticism. It often quotes and enforces rules for behaving and relating, as well as other family traditions in much the same way actual parent figures used to do.

When Kennedy and Powers talked about how to rear their children, they were probably in their Parent ego states and expressing the same values that their own mothers and fathers did.

The Child ego state expresses feelings and emotions that were learned in childhood through parental training and personal experiences. Often in relationships the Child ego state shows itself when friends are compliant, rebellious, or manipulative, or, more positively, when they are intuitive, creative and sensitive to the needs and wishes of their friends. The Child ego state is also a source of a friend's desires for affection, fun and personal pleasure.

When Kennedy and Powers laughed together or had a drink, they were probably in their Child ego states.

The Adult ego state is called upon to think clearly and make rational decisions. Its judgments are based on objective facts, not just on parental tradition and opinions or on childlike feelings and conditioning.

When Kennedy and Powers analyzed the news, they were probably in their Adult ego states.

All three ego states are important in friendship.

Two friends, from their Adult ego states, may share a common intellectual interest or skill.

The same friends, from their Child ego states, may also enjoy a round of golf together.

From their concerned Parent, they may nurture each other in time of stress.

Affinity, or mutual attraction, that friends experience toward each other may well be based in some way on a certain compatibility between their ego states.

Ego States and Friendship

Berne claims that the essence of friendship is that there is "no active Parental ego state under ordinary conditions." He diagrams this as: [3]

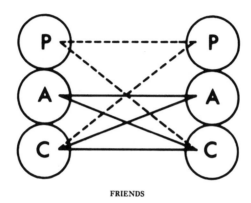

FRIENDS

Berne does not exclude the Parent ego state from friendship. He merely wants to emphasize that, as a rule, close friends do not criticize or punish each other as a parent might a child. Rather, when they do evaluate each other, it is done by offering information from an Adult ego state, not by handing down a condemnation from a punishing Parent ego state.

When friends take care of each other, as Powers did for Kennedy, the Parent ego state is important and essential. However, the Parent in third-self friendship is not overprotective and smothering, but nurturing and ready to help when necessary. True friends don't overhelp, they remain free and equal.

If overhelping or overcriticizing occurs in a friendship, the relationship loses its freedom. It becomes symbiotic with one

3. Eric Berne, *Sex in Human Loving* (New York: Grove Press), p. 137.

person constantly in the Parent ego state, the other constantly in the Child; or it breaks off.

Although Child and Parent ego states are often involved in friendships and may give the relationship its direction and energy, it is usually the friends' Adult ego states that freely make a commitment to friendship and keep the relationship from dying.

When two free and equal Adults are friends, they walk, symbolically, side by side. In friendships where one is Parent and the other Child, the Parent leads and the Child, symbolically, follows. Albert Camus asked for side-by-side friendship. He wrote,

> Don't walk in front of me,
> I may not follow.
> Don't walk behind me,
> I may not lead.
> Walk beside me,
> And just be my friend.

Leaving the Doll's House

Henrik Ibsen's play, *The Doll's House*, shows a Parent-to-Child relationship between Torvald and his sheltered wife, Nora. Torvald was both overly critical and overly protective. Nora remained an overly compliant Child.

But when a crisis emerged, she rebelled at staying in a Child-to-Parent relationship and declared her independence with:

Nora: . . . You have always been so kind to me but our home has been nothing but a playroom. I have been your doll-wife, just as at home I was papa's doll-child; and here the children have been my dolls. I thought it great fun when you played with me, just as they thought it great fun when I played with them. That is what our marriage has been, Torvald.

. . . .

I must stand quite alone, if I am to understand myself and everything about me. It is for that reason that I cannot remain with you any longer!

Torvald: Nora, Nora!

Nora: I am going away from here now, at once. . . .

Torvald: You are out of your mind! I won't allow it! I forbid you!

Nora: It is no use forbidding me anything any longer. I will take with me what belongs to myself. I will take nothing from you, either now or later.

Torvald: What sort of madness is this! [4]

Written at the turn of the century, this was a daring play, and Ibsen was one of the first to affirm the rights of women.

Currently, an increasing number of women are affirming their freedom and equality, and, in Nora's words, taking "what belongs to myself." In TA language, they wish to be recognized for having a thinking Adult ego state as well as a nurturing Parent and a sexy, fun-loving Child.

A growing number of men, too, desire to express all three ego states in their relationships. Wanting recognition for more than rational Adult thinking, they dress with color and flare, which lets others "see the child in me," and they assume jobs that have been traditionally labeled as nurturing women's work. In divorce cases, many men are receiving custody of their children. "I can do it as well as she," they maintain from their Parent.

Men and women today have more options for freely transacting with each other than when they were stuck in traditional roles of "husband" and "wife" or "man" and "woman."

Learning from Mom and Dad

Childhood experiences of friendship, or the lack of them, affect the kinds of friendships people develop later in life. Children who have satisfying friendships with moms and dads and peers usually learn to trust their Child ego state. This inner

4. Henrik Ibsen, "A Doll's House," in *Three Plays by Ibsen* (New York: Dell Publishing Co., 1959), pp. 195–196.

sense of feeling OK motivates them toward enjoying more friends in later life.

Vice President Nelson Rockefeller enjoys a close and warm relationship with his young sons. His wife describes it,

> Whenever possible, Nelson and the boys say prayers together before breakfast, at which time they have the opportunity to discuss their mutual interests. . . . Nelson has always said that it is not the quantity of time that you can spend with your children so much as the quality of the relationship developed in the time available. He throws himself into the relationship intensively—as he does in all undertakings he considers vital.[5]

Parents like Happy and Nelson Rockefeller, who *have* friends and who *are* friends with each other and with their children, usually are good friendship models. They trust people and demonstrate that friends can agree and disagree and can make up after disagreements. Their words and actions imply the importance of friendships.

Children who lack this positive experience with their parents often begin to mistrust their Child ego state. This feeling of not being OK usually interferes with forming close friendships in later life.

As a child, Benito Mussolini's relationships with his parents were poor. According to a biographer, "He was whipped and bullied by his father, pampered and kissed too much by his mother. . . . He never loved deeply, never had a true friend." [6]

Parents without friends are poor models for children to imitate.

Such parents often interfere, both physically and psychologically, with the friendships their children naturally form with other children.

General George S. Patton spent the first twelve years of his

---

5. "Happy Rockefeller's Story," an interview with Lynda Johnson Robb, *Ladies Home Journal*, June 1975, p. 112.
6. George Seldes, *Sawdust Caesar* (New York: Harper & Row, 1935).

life on an 1800-acre ranch almost totally isolated from all but his mother, his overprotective father, and baby sister. In preparatory school, he was rejected by his peers. At West Point, he was described as stiffnecked, arrogant, and boastful. In the military, he felt out of place when there was no battle to fight.

His biographer wrote of him, "So he gained the generalship, the medals and the glory, but he was never to make many friends." [7]

Ever suspicious parents may jerk away their children from playing with another child, or restrict them to isolated play in the back yard, or frequently discount other people's children, saying, "Those children don't know how to play" or "Those children can't be trusted" or "Those children are naughty."

Poet Vachel Lindsay suffered the effects of a "smothering" mother.

> During childhood he was kept apart from other children who might be rowdy or dirty. His curls were uncut, he wore immaculate white piqué suits, and played with two sisters. . . . His mother wrote a children's play in which Vachel was cast in the role of Cupid.[8]

Vachel was forty-six (after his mother died) before he married. Relationships with men and women of his own generation were difficult and painful. He never forgot the days when the other boys at school would not play with him. In fact, these humiliating memories probably influenced his suicide.

Unfortunately, many parents give messages that lead their children into weak or unhealthy relationships. Later in life their children may become "loners" or seek out people as friends who are indifferent or demanding or critical.

7. William B. Mellor, *Patton: The Fighting Man* (New York: G. P. Putnam, 1946).
8. Victor and Mildred Goertzel, *Cradles of Eminence* (Boston: Little, Brown, 1961), p. 111.

In some cases, children do not always comply with what mom and dad say. Instead, they may rebel and deny pessimistic parental messages. For example, a child may discover that in spite of what mistrusting parents say and do, some people *are* trustworthy.

Likewise, a child of trusting parents may also discover that some people are not to be trusted.

Trusting parents usually encourage their children to have friendships by taking them to playgrounds, arranging neighborhood events, inviting other children over, and intervening in squabbles only if necessary.

Statesman Adlai Stevenson was brought up in an explosive but trusting and affectionate household. Both parents and grandparents enjoyed Adlai and his sister Elizabeth, and many models of friendship were available in the family.

Grandfather Stevenson used to coax the children into the library with milk and cookies, then read to them while they enjoyed their food.

With their mother, the children often took long nature walks.

And at the dinner table they made up stories. One parent, usually their father, would begin a story, and someone else would add to it. The story was passed all around until everyone was shouting with laughter. Adlai says of his father, "He was one of the funniest men I've ever known." [9]

Trusting parents respect their children's unique personalities and show it by the friendly ways they transact with them.

Lines of Communication

In all relationships, three kinds of transactions are common:

9. Noel F. Busch, *Adlai E. Stevenson of Illinois* (New York: Farrar, Straus, 1952).

complementary, crossed, and *ulterior.* Friends learn how to identify and use each kind.

A *complementary transaction* occurs when a message, sent from a specific ego state in one person, gets the expected response from a specific ego state in another. When one person says Hello and gets a response of Hello, that is a complementary transaction.

Complementary transactions, common in third-self friendships, can occur between any two ego states. Common ones are diagrammed on page 122.

When Adlai Stevenson's family were improvising a story together at dinner, they were probably all in their creative Child ego states.

In complementary transactions, the lines of communication are parallel. Sharing is open and can continue indefinitely, unless something else occurs. The "something else" may be a crossed transaction.

Crossed transactions occur when the expected response is not given. Instead of being parallel, the lines between the ego states cross, and communication breaks down. The person who is crossed may feel misunderstood, surprised or confused.

For years, Torvald and Nora's transactions were predictably complementary, until she became dissatisfied and gave an unexpected response which crossed the transaction. Torvald was startled and confused.

When a straightforward Adult-to-Adult question such as "What time is it?" is asked, and the response is either from a Child ego state, "Why ask me?" or from a Parent, "Why don't you get your own watch fixed?" the transaction is said to be crossed. Common crossed transactions are diagrammed on page 123.

In third-self friendships, crossed transactions may lead to stress, but not always. Among friends, crossed transactions are sometimes acceptable if used carefully.

For example, if a friend talks on and on, or speaks in unclear

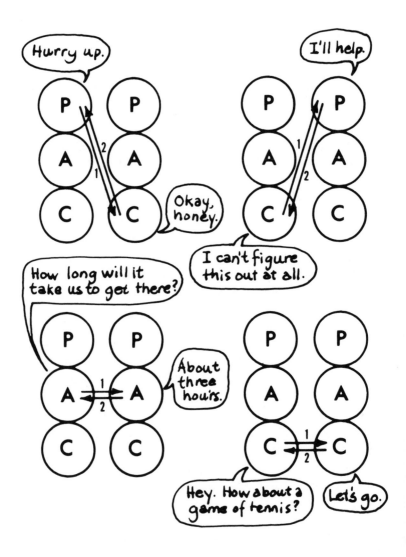

terms, or continually avoids solving a problem, an effective crossed transaction might be, "Hey, can I have a chance to talk now?" or "What do you expect of me when you tell me things over and over" or "Is there something you'd like to tell me but can't quite put into words?"

Friends learn to use crossed transactions in ways that do not demean each other.

The desire to be well liked and esteemed by others, to enjoy the depths or heights of friendship, is a fundamental aspect of being human. People reach out, wanting friends and friendship, hoping that others will also want them. Lines of communication are crucially important in friendship.

Sometimes crossed transactions create pressures and problems among friends.

Alan Paton described an almost tragic husband-and-wife relationship in *Too Late the Phalarope*. He told of Peeler, a policeman, who wrote to his wife about feelings he dared not yet express face to face.

> Perhaps one day when you are convinced, and know that my love of your body is part of my love of you yourself, and when you are no longer afraid of it, and accept it truly, and know that such love is no enemy, then perhaps I shall tell you more about myself, for you do not know it all. And if I knew your love was sure forever, I should not fear to tell you, in fact I should wish to tell you. Then our love would be complete, and nothing would be hidden by one from the other. . . . Then I would be in heaven, and safe from all the dangers I told you of, and the angers and ugly moods. . . .

His wife dismissed the invitation and closed the door to communication by crossing the transaction with:

> The long part of your letter I cannot answer fully now, but we shall talk about it when I get home. . . . As for these dangers, I think you imagine them, and they are not there at all.[11]

Ulterior transactions, those that have a hidden agenda, are more complex than the other two kinds since they involve more than two ego states at the same time.[12]

The old cliché "It's not what you say, it's the way that you say it" applies to ulterior transactions.

At the verbal level, in ulterior messages Adult ego states

11. Alan Paton, *Too Late the Phalarope* (New York: Charles Scribner's Sons, 1953), pp. 136–137.
12. Muriel James, *The OK Boss* (Reading, Mass.: Addison-Wesley, 1975).

"It's not what you say, it's the way that you say it"

appear to be in charge of the transaction (solid lines in diagram below). At the psychological level, other ego states convey the "real" message (dotted lines). An ulterior message may be pleasant or unpleasant.

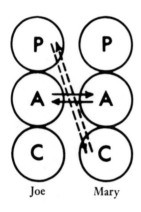

Joe   Mary

Joe: (frowning) "Do you notice the time?"

Mary: (anxiously) "Yes, it's 3 o'clock. I'm trying."

UNPLEASANT ULTERIOR TRANSACTION

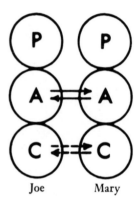

Joe   Mary

Joe: (smiling) "Want to see my etchings?"

Mary: (smiling) "I love etchings."

PLEASANT ULTERIOR TRANSACTION

In each case, on the verbal level, Joe's Adult seems to be asking a simple question and Mary's answer seems to be giving Adult information. However, the frown, the anxious tone of voice, the smiles are what convey the real messages of approval or disapproval.

In the first example, Mary probably feels put down by Joe's frown, and their third self of friendship, if it exists, may be threatened.

In the second example, Mary seems to be pleased. Here, their third self, if it exists, would be strengthened.

Ulterior messages are often given nonverbally, through body language, facial expression, or tone of voice. Whining, giggling and sarcastic tones all convey strong messages.

People use ulterior transactions because they are afraid to be open and honest about their own needs and their own perceptions of others.

As Shirley Maclaine said, "The more I travel, the more I realize that fear makes strangers of people who should be friends."

At times, close friends and third-self friends use ulterior transactions as stepping stones into intimacy.

Rex Stout, famous mystery writer, portrayed in his stories two friends who were masters of crossed and ulterior transactions.

One friend was immense, 285-pound Nero Wolfe, grand master of detection, woman-hater, connoisseur of fancy foods, and grower of rare orchids, who never left home, an old brownstone on West 35th Street in New York City.

The second friend, Wolfe's sidekick, was Archie Goodwin, a 178-pounder, who was always on the move meeting suspects and culling evidence.

Since detectives are expected to be highly rational, Wolfe's and Archie's transactions on the verbal level are clearly Adult. But because both of them have "egos" as big as Manhattan, the nonverbal message from both of them, on the psychological level, may often be described as a critical Parent talking down to a stupid Child. It might be diagrammed as on page 128.

Archie and Wolfe were inseparable friends and seemed to enjoy relating in this subtle way. For them, it was a pleasurable pastime.

Game Playing

Everyone plays psychological games. A game is a series of transactions with an emotional payoff. The heart of a game

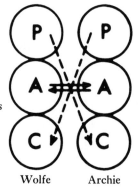

Without turning his head, Wolfe let out a growl ... and demanded, "Who is Miss Blount?"

Archie tightened his lips and then parted them to say ..., "She has an appointment with you at eleven-thirty, as you know." [13]

Wolfe   Archie

is an ulterior transaction. A game ends with someone feeling badly. Later, these negative feelings may be "cashed in" for "prizes." For example, a game's outcome may justify one friend in having a crying jag and another in throwing a temper tantrum. If after any series of transactions, one or both friends feel badly, a game has probably been played.

Friends are seldom aware that they are into a game until the game is over. Awareness usually dawns when they feel not-OK in some way, or when one friend feels self-righteous and the other feels badly.

Among friends, games are often repetitive. The same game is played over and over again, with the players remarking, "It seems as if we've been through this before."

There are many games friends play.

Each game has a theme from which it gets its name. Common games easily recognized are:

NAME OF THE GAME	THEME OF THE GAME
Harried	Being "too busy" and having no time to develop closeness

13. Rex Stout, *Gambit: A Nero Wolfe Novel* (New York: Viking, 1962), p. 1. Text slightly adapted.

Kick Me	Continually doing things to get a friend's disapproval
Poor Me	Complaining and complaining to get sympathy
Why Don't You	Giving more and more advice that is not wanted
I'm Only Trying to Help You	Continually being available, but only to help
Blemish	Being a nit-picker, finding all the little things that are wrong
Now I've Got You	Being distrustful; waiting for a friend to make an error, then pouncing on him or her

Games are played at various levels of intensity. Big game players, like Patton or Mussolini, may end up with a big "prize" of homicide or suicide. Less serious players may feel justified in quitting a friendship. Small game players usually end up simply feeling badly. If this happens frequently, a third self does not develop.

It is not necessary to know the name of the game as long as "the game plan" is known. To discover a game plan, the following questions are asked:

> What keeps happening over and over in our friendship that leaves either of us feeling badly?
>
> How does it start?
>
> What happens next? And next?
>
> How does it all end?
>
> How does each friend feel when it ends? [14]

Nora recognized the game plan that she and Torvald had

14. John James, "The Game Plan," *Transactional Analysis Bulletin*, Vol. 3, No. 4 (October 1973), pp. 14–17. Also see, Muriel James and Dorothy Jongeward, *The People Book* (Reading, Mass.: Addison-Wesley, 1975), pp. 134–135.

been playing—Torvald was the overprotective Parent, she was the sheltered Child, and the name of their game was *The Doll's House.*

"I have been your doll-wife, just as at home I was papa's doll-child," Nora explained. "That is what our marriage has been, Torvald."

She saw how the game started, what happened time after time, and how it would all end. She didn't like the helpless feeling of always being the Child, so she decided to break up the game.

Breaking Up Games

From time to time, casual friends, even close friends, need to break up the games they're playing. There are several options.

The first would be to *withdraw* from the relationship, either physically or psychologically, verbally or nonverbally. Many marital divorces are a form of this first option.

In general, a withdrawing person might say something like, "I don't think our relationship now is constructive for us" or "Perhaps we need some distance from each other for awhile." This means, "I don't care to play this game any longer."

A second option for breaking up games involves *crossing* the game transaction when it occurs. Nora used this option with Torvald, as well as withdrawing from the doll house.

To take another example, suppose one person craves an undue amount of sympathy and uses the game of "Poor Me" to elicit it. To cross this request, a friend might say, "I can't meet your need at this time" or "I feel as though you want sympathy from me now, but I don't wish to give it." A less direct response would be, "I'm changing some things in my life so I probably won't be able to see you as often as I have in the past."

A third and better game-breaking option would be simply

to *bypass* a repetitive game and work directly for the positive payoff that each player really wants.

For example, friends who really want warmth and tenderness from each other may begin by playing a loud game of "Uproar." This game requires each player to criticize the other, taking turns, each criticism spoken in a louder voice than the one before. The game ends when the friends feel hurt and angry toward each other.

Later, in order to remove the hurt and angry feelings, they may make up with warmth and tenderness, which is precisely the positive payoff they wanted in the first place but didn't know how to get directly.[15]

By becoming aware of the games they play, close friends can learn how to get the positive payoffs they seek without playing hurtful games with each other.

Scripts People Act Out

Everyone has a psychological script. Much like a theatrical script, it involves a theme, a plot, cast of characters, dialogue, producer, a stage, scenery and acts. It is a lifetime story of which the beginning, middle and ending are already written.

Psychological scripts are like dramas that people feel compelled to act out year after year.

Games are small scenes in the total drama. People play their games and live by their scripts, seldom knowing that they do so.

Eric Berne said a person who is living out a script and unaware of it is like

> someone at a player piano, acting as though the music is his creation, and sometimes rising to take a bow or a boo from his friends and relatives, who also believe he is playing his own tune.[16]

15. John James, "Positive Payoff after Games," *Transactional Analysis Journal*, 1976.
16. Eric Berne, *What Do You Say after You Say Hello?* (New York: Grove Press, n.d.), p. 244.

On June 10, 1922, Frances Ethel Gumm was born. In childhood she dreamed about a life of love, magic, glamour, excitement. She wanted to wrap her arms around the world and have the world wrap its arms around her. And it all happened. The script played perfectly, for the Frances Gumm of childhood became the grownup Judy Garland.

Her biographer summed up Judy's script.

> Seeking love, she had many men, yet she had never found it; for finding it, she could not believe it; or if she believed it, suspected it; or suspecting it, denied it. Frances Gumm. Judy Garland. Was there ever a Judy Garland? Was it not all Frances Gumm, endlessly playing the part, endlessly in search of herself?[17]

The scripts people act out may resemble a trite soap opera, an interesting saga, a tragedy, a farce, a romance, a comedy, or a dull play that bores the players and would put an audience to sleep.[18]

Television shows sometimes captivate viewers because characters act out scripts that people recognize.

Without admitting it, many men probably identify with cigar-smoking Archie Bunker who plays out the script of the self-centered, prejudiced American grownup.

Or they see themselves in loser Bob Newhart who is scripted as the bungling, stuttering professional who seems to need more psychological help than his patients.

Or they feel right at home with the Jeffersons, an eternally bickering couple with a complaining mother-in-law.

Television allows viewers to explore in fantasy scripts that they could never live in real life.

Many women might envy Mary Tyler Moore who happily bounces through a day in the exciting romantic life of the as-

17. Gerold Frank, *Judy* (New York: Harper & Row, 1975).
18. Muriel James and Dorothy Jongeward, *Born to Win: Transactional Analysis and Gestalt Experiments* (Reading, Mass.: Addison-Wesley, 1971), pp. 68–100.

yet-unattached young working woman, a friend to all the men and women in her life.

Others might imagine being like Zsa Zsa Gabor, who has been scripted as the middle-aged woman who seems to remain eternally young and attractive to men.

Men might fantasize themselves in the roles of Kojak, Mannix, or other crimestoppers scripted as hardnosed cops who relate to people with an unbeatable combination of muscles, brains and hearts of gold. Or, identify more with the middleaged Dean Martin surrounded by young women.

Avid television-watchers, children see all these scripts and those of their parents lived out day after day before their eyes.

Drama Stages for Friendship

The types of scripts people act out can be classified as *constructive, destructive,* or as banal and *going nowhere.*

Infants in a family are usually the "center of attention." They are placed in the spotlight, at the front of the stage, hopefully being applauded by their family. In this way a constructive life-script starts to develop.

A *constructive* script is one of continuing growth. Challenges are faced and overcome. People in constructive scripts care about themselves and others. They care about the world in which they live. They make friends with different kinds of peoples and treasure the friendships they make.

If children are pushed out of the spotlight prematurely by another child being born, or by another family member in some kind of crisis, they may decide they'll never make it. They may live a life drama as though on a treadmill that *goes nowhere.* Their friendships may be only casual because they are afraid to risk closeness.

In some families, children receive little positive "audience" response. They may select or be assigned lines and actions in a drama that leads to a *destructive* ending. Ronald was like that. He and his sister were friends but were scripted for tragedy.

At age twenty-five, Ronald hanged himself. He had devoted his life to caring for his ailing twin sister, and when she died at age eighteen he had nothing to live for. He became increasingly depressed and withdrawn. In discussing Ronald's suicide, his parents said:

> *Mother:* I'm not surprised. It was inevitable. We've had several suicides in our family over the years. In fact, my brother slit his own throat. I warned Ronnie many times he might kill himself. Even his sister wouldn't take her medicine. No wonder she died so young.

> *Father:* All my life I have felt defeated and gloomy. In fact, my father owned a funeral parlor. When Ronnie would ask me for advice, I tried hard not to give it to him and would just quote the parables of Jesus. What else could I have done? For years I've been depressed and have drunk myself off two jobs. Guess I haven't been too good an example. Maybe Ronnie's way wasn't so bad.[19]

A destructive script demeans or destroys one or more of the players. Children physically brutalized or ignored in childhood, or others who have friendships with parents or peers that end in tragedy, may unknowingly expect a replay of a similar tragedy in later life.

People with destructive scripts may break up a friendship over a minor matter and stay angry or depressed about it for years.

Identifying Scripts

One way to identify either a personal script or a friendship script is by asking questions.

To identify the action, ask, "What happens to people like me?" and "What happens to friendships like ours?"

19. *Ibid.*, p. 82.

To find a script theme, ask, "Does my personal script seem to be constructive, destructive or going nowhere?" "What keeps happening over and over again like a theme in my friendships?" "What might the audience say about my character in the play?"

To become aware of the final curtain, ask, "If I go on as I now am, what will be the logical conclusions?" or "If our friendship goes on as it now is, what will be the logical conclusions?"

Another way for friends to identify their friendship script is to view themselves as characters on stage, and ask, "What seems to be going on?" "Where is the plot taking us?" "Is the action satisfying?" "Who's enjoying it?"

To summarize each different period of a friendship, it's interesting to sketch a stage and also to draw the people who were on stage at the time. The places these people took and their actions on stage may reveal patterns that helped or hindered close and third-self friendships.

Some scripts are like fairy tales or children's stories people once heard and decided to live by. Knowing someone's favorite childhood story often reveals a basic theme in their life.

For example, like Chicken Little, they may continually fear that something terrible is going to happen.

Or, like the Woman Who Lived in a Shoe, they may always feel overwhelmed and frustrated by life's daily problems.

Or, like Cinderella, they may nourish the hope of meeting, marrying and living "happily ever after."

Or, like the Gingerbread Boy, may tantalize others into endlessly chasing after them.

Rewriting a Script

A script that is destructive or banal and going nowhere can be "rewritten" by redecisions.

For example, suspicious people, like a man who continually sings "I Wonder Who's Kissing Her Now?" may have decided in childhood that women can't be trusted. Such men need to redecide in favor of trusting some women.

Some people believe the song, "You Always Hurt the One You Love." Others believe just the opposite and decide that everyone is out to hurt them. They may need to redecide in favor of standing up for themselves to avoid being hurt. Or they may need to select gentle, not hurtful, friends.

Many people decide that they won't love anyone again because in childhood a special friend went away. This script is reflected in songs like, "When Your Lover Has Gone" or "I'll Never Fall in Love Again" or "Alone Again, Naturally." Such people need to redecide in favor of love even if separation is inevitable.

Peggy Lee's song hit "Is That All There Is?" points to people who decide that life is a drag or that there's "no use trying." Such people may need to redecide in favor of a life that can be beautiful and in experimenting with new ways of relating that are likely to be successful.

Redecisions are not easy. It may take years to change a destructive life script that was adopted in childhood.

Filmstar Anthony Quinn was scripted early in life to an almost insatiable desire for power and superiority.

On his first visit to a psychiatrist, Quinn explained his destructive script by recalling an anecdote often told in his family about the proud Mexican revolutionary leader Pancho Villa and his legendary thirst for power and superiority.

> Villa rode to the top of the hill and saw the Pacific Ocean for the first time.

> He had stared at the ocean's immensity for many minutes without saying a word. Then he'd reined his horse and started back down the hill.

> His lieutenant, riding behind him, said, "Quite a sight, eh, Jefe?"

"It's too small to quench my thirst," Pancho said over his shoulder.[20]

Mr. Quinn admitted that he, like Pancho Villa, had similar problems trying to quench his thirst for power, and he spent many years working with his psychiatrist to overcome his destructive script.

Time for Friendship

Transactional Analysis lists six ways people, including friends, structure their time. Each way may be used or abused.

First, people may *withdraw* from others, either physically by leaving the situation, or psychologically by reading the newspaper, answering the phone, engaging in daydreams, or watching TV.

Since everyone needs privacy and time to be alone, withdrawing is often useful. It is necessary for personal development. However, to remain alone when the world calls with its many offers of friendship is a tragedy. Eleanor Roosevelt, writing of her years in Washington, says:

> On the whole, however, I think I lived those years very impersonally. It was almost as though I had erected someone a little outside of myself who was the President's wife. I was lost somewhere deep down inside myself. That is the way I felt and worked until I left the White House.[21]

Although having a third self deepens the meaning of life and may enhance moments of solitude, withdrawal can also be an abuse of friendship.

This may happen if a close friend withdraws too often, or for extended periods of time without telling the other friend why, or withdraws during crises when the presence of both persons is needed.

20. Anthony Quinn, *The Original Sin: A Self-Portrait* (Boston: Little, Brown, 1972), p. 10.
21. Anna Eleanor Roosevelt, *This I Remember* (New York: Harper & Row, 1949), pp. 350–351.

The second way friends may spend time together is in *rituals*. These are stereotyped transactions, like Hello and Goodbye, that often serve to get an acquaintanceship started.

Alice had been taught the polite rituals that a little girl should know, but she sometimes forgot them in her wanderings through Wonderland.

> "You've begun wrong!" cried Tweedledum. "The first thing in a visit is to say 'How d'ye do?' and shake hands!" And here the two brothers gave each other a hug, and then they held out the two hands that were free, to shake hands with her.
>
> Alice did not like shaking hands with either of them first, for fear of hurting the other one's feelings; so, as the best way out of the difficulty, she took hold of both hands at once: the next moment they were dancing in a ring.[22]

Rituals are minimal greetings of courtesy that provide some recognition and keep the social wheels greased.

The abuse of rituals occurs when friends, especially those who live together, use rituals to avoid moving toward deeper relationship levels, or when one friend refuses to participate in the rituals that have meaning to the other friend.

A third way people spend time together is with *pastimes*. These are often pleasant conversations about subjects such as cars, sporting events, clothes and so forth. They are useful to casual friends who wonder about whether or not they wish a more intensive encounter, and to friends who have been out of communication for awhile and want to "catch up" on what each has been doing.

As with rituals, an abuse occurs when friendships that could be close remain at a pastime level, the friends refusing to reveal anything of significance about themselves to each other.

A fourth way to structure time involves playing *psychologi-*

---

22. Lewis Carroll, *Through the Looking Glass* (Lancer ed., 1968), p. 186.

cal games. All people play games—some play harder than others—yet people are seldom aware of their games.

Ulterior games are always an abuse of any relationship and, if consistently played, may prevent a healthy third self from developing, or may eventually destroy one that has evolved.

Fifth, friends may spend time together in *activities,* often called work. Activities might include planning a joint project, working in the garden, balancing a checkbook. Activities provide a matrix in which friendships may be conceived. Activities may also be the common interests that hold friends together and stimulate friendships to further growth.

However, if friends are always working apart, or if one friend constantly works and the other doesn't, there is little time to develop a third self.

Sixth, *intimacy* is always a prerequisite for close friendships and for a third self. Intimacy develops in feelings of trust, openness, affection and appreciation. Feelings of intimacy may be recognized in the middle of a joint activity or at its successful conclusion. Intimacy is not the same as a sexual attraction although it may include that.

Third-self intimacy normally involves the meeting of many psychic layers. It involves the encounter of ideas, skills or interests in an atmosphere of belongingness and mutual esteem.

Intimacy often takes time to develop, especially if the people involved come from very different backgrounds as in the case of Nancy and Henry Kissinger.

Politically, she was a devoted Rockefeller team member; he was strongly in the Nixon camp. Religiously, he was a German Jew whose parents were strongly orthodox; she was a Christian in a long tradition of Christians. Their backgrounds were radically different. He was a foreigner, an immigrant, a divorced "swinger," who lacked her social grace and Establishment manners. She was a Westchester WASP, the daughter of a prominent New York lawyer.

Each of the conflicts had to be faced and worked through. The friendship took almost ten years to mature fully.

Slowly, in 1968, after four years of isolated meetings and what Nancy described as "chattering" about politics—"We have always been chatterers"—the two began meeting each other more often. Mutual interests began to increase—"long walks down Fifth Avenue, Marx Brothers movies on the upper West Side, Westerns on the *Late Show*." More seriously, they attended seminars together on European politics, Vietnam, Soviet-American relations.

"A stimulating, easy rapport developed, a bond of mutual respect and affection grew," Mrs. Kissinger recalled. "It was *such* a gradual process. It just grew. It takes time for two people to get close to each other." [23]

Prime Time

People in third-self friendships always find time for each other.

Time spent with a friend is called *kairos*, a Greek word meaning "special time" or "meaning-filled time." It is not time measured by a clock, but by the significance of the event.

Time spent with acquaintances or casual friends involves *chronos*, a Greek word meaning "clock-measured time." People who are caught up in *chronos* are usually more concerned with the quantity of minutes and hours they spend with somebody than with the quality or meaning of what they do together.

Yet, it is not necessarily the *quantity* of time people spend with each other as much as the *quality* of the time spent that enhances a relationship.

Close friends like to save prime time for being together. This is different from "leftover" time—when friends may be too tired to give much of themselves.

23. See Marvin Kalb, "Nancy Kissinger: My Life with Henry," *Ladies Home Journal*, April 1975, p. 75.

Many friendships stay at a superficial level because friends do not save prime time for each other. In such cases the potential third self, lacking nourishment, may never develop. Friends may recognize the symptoms and say things like, "But you never have time for me" or "Whenever we're together you're too tired to enjoy it."

While some people describe being with others as "wasting time" or "killing time," close friends and third-self friends "treasure" their time together. They treasure the challenges which call for their authentic responses.[24] For them, time together is filled with meaning, and it contributes to the development of the new third self. As the Little Prince tells the fox, each rose is unique, and "It is the time you have wasted for your rose that makes your rose so important."

The New Third Self

Close friendships require intimacy. They require a candid person-to-person relationship of openness and trust, without exploitation and without the psychological games that people usually play.

A third self of friendship requires even more. Each friend contributes to the new friendship entity, even as each parent does to the forming of a new child.

Neither friend stays encapsulated "because of fear, guilt, resentment, disinterest, or because they were adapted in childhood to 'keep their distance.' "[25]

Rather, the friends are open and in dialogue with each other. Both give of their essence, or inner core. This essence is fused into a third self, an entity which cannot be seen but is nevertheless there. In the words of the fox to the Little Prince, "It is only with the heart that one can see rightly; what is essential is invisible to the eye."

Since a third self is an entity independent of the two friends,

24. Muriel James, *Born to Love: Transactional Analysis in the Church* (Reading, Mass.: Addison-Wesley, 1973), pp. 170–171.
25. *Ibid.*, p. 185.

and, in a sense, enjoys its own life, energy and personality, a third self of friendship could be diagrammed in the following way.

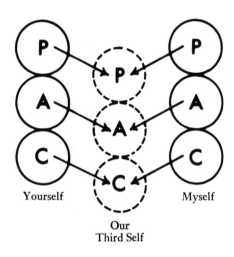

Yourself

Myself

Our
Third Self

The caring characteristics of each friend's Parent ego state, the mutual interests and skills of each friend's Adult, the warmth, openness, and creativity of each friend's Child combine to form a new metaperson, the third self.

At an even deeper level, the third self manifests a sharing of inner-core energies from each of the friends.[26] It points to a fusion of a love-power between friends that lies beneath the observable expressions of Parent, Adult and Child ego states.

It is as if love-energy from the inner core of one friend reaches out to love-energy from the inner core of the other, and the two love-energies fuse into a new unity, which becomes a new entity, a third self of friendship.

26. For a discussion of the TA concepts *inner core* and *the power within*, see Muriel James and Louis M. Savary, *The Power at the Bottom of the Well: Transactional Analysis and Religious Experience* (New York: Harper & Row, 1974), pp. 17–27.

From birth, these love-energies in people continually reach out in order to form unities in friendship.

So it is, the exploration of friendship that begins at birth is a lifelong process. And, wrote T. S. Eliot, "the end of all our exploring will be to arrive where we started and know the place for the first time."

⤚§ 8 §⤙

The Art of Friendship

Every artist was once an amateur.
RALPH WALDO EMERSON

Friendship Potential

Everyone is gifted with the potential for developing strong friendships and can become skilled at this art.

It is relatively easy to attract others or be attracted by them so that an initial relationship can develop. It takes an artist to keep the process going so that new levels of friendship continue to be experienced.

"If friendship were easy, there would be a lot more of it in the world," claimed Andrew Greeley.

Since people may also lose important friendships by mistreating or ignoring them, friendships need tender loving care and frequent repairs.

Here's where the art of friendship enters in.

Defining Art

In the public library's reference room, the card catalogue under "Arts of" and "Arts and Crafts of" lists well over a hundred different forms of art. Arts run from the beginning of the alphabet—advertising, advocacy, ancestor hunting—to the end of it—wood-turning, yodeling, zoo-keeping. The list includes scores of fine arts, performing arts and vocational arts. It seems that any area of human concern offers people the chance to grow from amateurs to artists.

Picasso, painter-sculptor especially known for his development of cubist art, was once asked, "What is art?"

He replied, "And what is not art?" [11]

Rodin points out that for him art is not just painting or sculpting, but many things all at once.

> Art is contemplation. It is the pleasure of the mind. . . . It is the joy of the intellect. . . . Art is the most sublime mission of man. . . . Art, moreover, is taste. It is a reflection of the artist's heart. . . .[2]

There is an art of architecture, of painting, of sculpting, of drawing, of acting, of dancing. There is an art of politics as well as an art of city planning. There is an art of crafting and an art of living as well as an art of friendship.[3]

Aristotle once wrote,

> The business of every art is to bring something into existence, and the practice of any art involves studying how to bring this something into existence.

In the art of painting, the business is to bring a painting into existence; in architecture, a building; in poetry, a poem; in music, a song; in ballet, a dance. Friendship artists bring a third self of friendship into existence.

Requirements of Friendship

Erich Fromm claims that "the practice of any art has certain general requirements, quite regardless of whether we deal with the art of carpentry, medicine, or the art of love." [4]

1. Jaime Sabartes, *Picasso: An Intimate Portrait,* trans. Angel Flores (Englewood Cliffs, N.J.: Prentice-Hall, 1948), p. 206.
2. Auguste Rodin, *On Art & Artists* (New York: Philosophical Library, 1957), pp. 29-30.
3. See Joseph Hudnut, *Architecture and the Spirit of Man* (Cambridge: Harvard University Press, 1949); also, Walter Sorell, *The Dance Has Many Faces* (New York: Columbia University Press, 1966).
4. Erich Fromm, *The Art of Loving* (New York: Bantam Books), p. 90.

"The practice of any art involves studying how to bring this something into existence"

The four requirements Fromm lists are *discipline, concentration, patience* and *ultimate concern.* These same requirements apply to the art of friendship.

Do these requirements sound pretty heavy? Like parental advice? Shouldn't friendship be fun instead of work?

A moment's reflection will reveal that people frequently employ these four qualities. For example, when preparing for a party, a woman might use *discipline* when putting on makeup, might *concentrate* on each detail, *patiently* apply eyeliner and shadow, and be very *concerned* with the ultimate result.

At the party, she probably enjoys herself a bit more because she is confident that she looks her best. She has met Fromm's four requirements in practicing the art of using cosmetics.

Each woman remembers the first time she applied cosmetics; the result was probably more like an amateur experiment with paints, powders and liquids than a work of art. But with discipline, concentration, patience and ultimate concern, her cosmetic skill improved. And through practice she developed from amateur to artist.

Discipline

People do not become artists unless they use self-discipline.

Interpretive singer Peggy Lee is an artist with discipline. Painstaking professionalism characterizes her. "Preparation is the whole thing," is the way she explains her success.

Since the early 1940s when she made her first hit with the Benny Goodman Band, Peggy has carried a small black notebook.

"That's my show book," she explains. It is full of detailed notes and bits of data. Every show she has done for decades is carefully recorded, each song she sang and what she wore, the lighting, the music and the audience. For upcoming shows, Peggy's book outlines, even to hand gestures, what is to happen on stage during her show. She marks down the numbers she will sing with detailed comments on treatment, reminding herself to ask for "more guitar here, or less of the French horn here."

"It's a very organized little book," she says.[5]

Although they may not need a detailed Peggy Lee show-book, friends can take time to observe closely the ingredients that may have fostered success in their friendship.

They can notice the experiences, conversations and shared ideas that helped to strengthen and enrich their third self. They can take note of their mistakes in relating, and agree to avoid them in the future. They can discuss alternative ways of responding to difficult situations, or brush up on communication skills, or decide to add new ingredients, such as tennis or symphonic music, to their relationship.

In transactional analysis terms, self-control and discipline are activities of the Adult ego state. Friendships in which the Adult is healthy and strong are likely to report a lot of thinking, planning and useful decisions. The Adult ego state acts as guide for the third self in its growth.

An art implies rules, patterns and objectives. Finding a friend, developing a third self, maintaining it in an ever-changing process, and growing with it demand much self-control.

Baseball's Hank Aaron, who surpassed Babe Ruth's homerun record, is almost glacially cool on the diamond. For the quiet black superstar from Alabama, baseball is his art, and to be an artist on the playing field requires discipline.

"Hitting," he insists, "is mostly *thinking*."

At bat in tense situations, before 50,000 screaming spectators, Aaron seems relaxed. When he steps to the plate, his mind is racing. He memory-banks every pitcher's pitch. He claims he can recall specific throws served up to him years ago.

5. Henry Pleasants, *The Great American Popular Singers* (New York: Simon & Schuster, 1974), p. 346.

For individual pitchers, he is often able to compute what's coming next.[6]

Those who practice their art only when they are "in the mood" may develop an enjoyable hobby but they do not become masters of the art.

Sometimes when they're "not in the mood," friends may ignore the courtesies and contacts that cement friendship, saying to themselves, "Oh well, he's my friend. He'll understand."

Although this careless style of relating may be tolerated—even expected—the richness possible in authentic art does not develop. Maintaining friends requires self-discipline.

Discipline is seen in friends who take time to make a phone call or write a note or send a gift or meet for coffee. It is evident in friends who have learned how to say the right thing and when to say it and in the friends who have learned from their mistakes to act in ways that enrich all three selves in a friendship.

Concentration

Concentration, another requirement for the art of friendship, involves focusing on the relationship, making the third self the center of attention. It means being able to listen, to live fully in the present and to be sensitive to oneself, to the friend and to the relationship. Concentration allows a friendship's intensity to grow and its depth to increase.

"But," said Ann to Sarah, "I really don't want to come to your Saturday-night party."

"Why?" asked Sarah, disappointed.

"Because our friendship is too important to me."

"I don't understand," replied Sarah puzzled.

6. David MacDonald, "Henry Aaron, Superstar," *Kansas City Star Magazine*, March 10, 1974.

"Every time I come to one of your big parties—and they're the only kind you've been having—I feel like a piece of wall-paper. You're always so busy in the kitchen, waiting on everybody, making jokes, running around, that about all I get from you is 'Hello, how are you?' and 'Goodbye.' "

"But I want you to like all my friends."

"Look, Sarah, I guess your friends are okay, but I've never shared a meaningful experience with them as I have with you."

"Can't you come to the party just to have fun? Everybody needs some laughs and jokes now and then."

"Sure, Sarah. And I do, too. But you and I so seldom find time to be together to keep our friendship alive. That's what I miss."

"I guess I miss it too," Sarah replied after a pause.

"I'd rather spend our time together in a smaller group or just the two of us alone, when we can both concentrate on what-ever it is we're talking about."

The diluted attention Ann expected from Sarah at the party would lead to resentment. Ann viewed their friendship as something special and wanted to focus on it. When the focus was missing, Ann tended to feel left out, depressed or even hostile at times.

Concentration suffers when attention is *distracted* or *diluted* by a number of interests.

It is common for people in contemporary culture to try to do many things at once—talk, eat and watch television simul-taneously. Some men listen to music and shave with a cord-less shaver while driving to work. Some women cook lunch and talk to friends on the phone while disciplining the chil-dren. Some people invite their business associates and "best" friends to a party, hoping to enjoy each one individually and hoping that each one will enjoy the others collectively. In-stead, people make only surface contact.

"The excellence of every art is its intensity," wrote poet John Keats.

Concentration, or intensity, in friendship is usually diluted when other people, especially more than a few, enter the situation.

From childhood, Norman Rockwell concentrated on his art. Once described as the man who drew "women you wished your son would marry," he began his art early and came up the hard way. The illustrator, who did over three hundred covers for *The Saturday Evening Post,* was born near the turn of the century in the back bedroom of a shabby New York City brownstone building on 103rd Street and Amsterdam Avenue.

> When I was six or seven years old, I used to draw ships on pieces of cardboard for my brother and another boy. . . . I sketched dogs, houses and vegetables, and, from my imagination, pirates, whales, Indians. I drew pictures of the characters from Dickens. I found I liked to draw.[7]

Like illustrators, trapeze artists are another group who must be disciplined and concentrated. Brothers Tito and Armando Gaona with their sister, Chela, began practicing at age five. By twelve, they were trapeze pros. Recently, after a week of competitive judging by circus experts, they were awarded the Circus Oscar in Madrid as "the best flying act in the world." Few circus flying teams try the triple somersault in the big tent, but Tito can do it *blindfolded.*[8]

Patience

"Success is one percent inspiration and ninety-nine percent perspiration," said inventor Thomas A. Edison. A practical, hard-headed New Jersey man, Edison depended for success less

7. Norman Rockwell, *My Adventures as an Illustrator* (New York: Doubleday, 1960).
8. William Johnson, "Most Daring Young Man on the Flying Trapeze," *Sports Illustrated,* April 8, 1974.

"The excellence of every art is its intensity"

upon genius than upon native common sense and a tremendous capacity for patient work. By the end of his life, he had been granted nearly 1,100 patents for his different inventions.

Patience is also a requirement for building successful friendships.

An uncommon virtue among people who are always in a hurry, patience seems a drawback for those who want to get somewhere quickly, who want to read complicated ideas in simple digest form, who seldom want to take time to talk things out. Patience is a word that is seldom used in an "I want it *now*" culture.

Although there may be a quick initial attraction between two people, a growing friendship can't be rushed.

Ivan, a college student, came in for counseling.

> I just don't understand Judy. She's so intense I almost feel like running in the opposite direction these days when I see her. We've only had three dates. She's intelligent, and when I first met her I was really turned on just talking to her about politics. But now all she wants to talk about is *feelings*. Her feelings about everything that happened to her in the past.
>
> I seem to want the relationship to go in a different direction. Actually, I want to talk about politics, not about feelings. I've told Judy so, but she won't take "no" for an answer. I guess if she keeps on pushing me, I'm going to back off. She wants too much instant intimacy and wants it too fast for me.

Friendships that rush into intimacy are seldom lasting ones. Like plants that are overfertilized, they may be lovely but short-lived. George Washington once described friendship as "a plant of slow growth."

Patience is needed to develop a root system of depth that can endure trials and tribulations. This is as true for friendships as it is for plants.

Grandmothers and grandfathers seem instinctively to understand the need for patience in relating to young children. Many children enjoy lovely friendships with grandparents.

Willie Morris, former editor-in-chief of *Harper's Magazine*, described his grandmother as "my favorite human being."

> When I was a boy, she and I took long walks around town in the gold summer dusk, out to the cemetery or miles and miles to the Old Ladies' Home, talking in torrents between the long silences.[9]

Grandmother Mamie wore a flowing dress and straw hat, and Willie went barefoot in a T-shirt and blue jeans with a sailor's cap on his head. "It was the years between us that made us close," Morris recalled.

With endless patience, she always tried to answer his questions, no matter how difficult they might be. "What are hills?" "How old are horses?" "Where do people go when they die?"

Friends can learn a lot about patience from people like Willie Morris's grandmother, and from young children like unconquerable Karen DeBolt.

"Daddy, will you stand at the top of the stairs? I want to try something," six-year-old Karen asked her father when he came home from work.

"Sure, honey," Robert DeBolt replied.

A child born without arms or legs, Karen had been patiently practicing for this moment since age two. Using her plastic arms and legs, supported by her favorite red, white and blue crutch, she began climbing up the twenty steps of the De-Bolt's circular stairway, pulling, heaving, and willing herself from one step to the next.

Triumphantly, she made it to the top and fell, laughing and crying, into her father's arms. Her brothers and sisters hugged and congratulated her.

For Karen, nothing seemed impossible as long as she was surrounded by the loving friendship of her family. Patiently, this multihandicapped child kept finding ways to do every-

9. Willie Morris, "Weep No More, My Lady," *Reader's Digest*, October 1974, p. 102.

thing she set her mind to. And patiently her family waited and welcomed each victory.[10]

Ultimate Concern

Ultimate concern is a fourth requirement for the growth of relationships in depth, length and meaning. To become artists at anything, people need to set their priorities so that they have a *supreme concern* with the mastery of the art. Fromm claims:

> If the art is not something of supreme importance, the apprentice, will never learn it. He will remain, at best, a good dilettante, but will never become a master.[11]

For Hippocrates, "Father of Medicine," his work was an art at the deepest level of experience. The ancient Greek physician organized the medical science of his time and wrote the famed Hippocratic Oath, to which thousands of physicians have since sworn loyalty, which calls for total personal involvement. Included in the oath are the lines, "I will lead my life and practice my art in uprightness and honor," and "I will exercise my art solely for the cure of my patient."

Those who see friendship as vitally important need to focus attention on their friendships with the ultimate concern of an artist. Ultimate concern involves faith. Friends need to be faithful to themselves and to each other. This often takes courage and risk. In friendship, there is no insurance against failure, pain or disappointment.

Usually, ultimate concern makes itself known in the small details of daily life. But in some situations the challenge of concern shows itself in the willingness to sacrifice oneself.

Third-self friendship grew up between detective-story writer Dashiell Hammett, author of *The Maltese Falcon* and *The Thin Man,* and Lillian Hellman, often called America's num-

10. Lynn Thomas, "Unconquerable Karen," *Ebony,* February 1974.
11. Erich Fromm, *The Art of Loving* (New York: Harper & Row, 1956), p. 92.

ber-one woman playwright and best known for her plays *The Children's Hour* and *The Little Foxes*.

Both writers were interested in civil rights and valued freedom of speech. When Hammett refused to give information to the House Un-American Activities Committee in 1951, he was jailed. After this, many of his so-called friends refused to associate with him. But Lillian Hellman stood up for him. And when he was released, she moved with him to Martha's Vineyard, so he could continue writing. There she protected him, now an invalid, from would-be intruders and interviewers until his death.

"Greater love has no man than this," said Jesus to his followers, "that a man lay down his life for a friend." This happens. During catastrophes some people are willing to risk their lives to pull a friend to safety.

Ultimate concern happens in some families or among friends when one person donates a kidney to save the life of another.

Or, someone will sacrifice their own chances for higher education and work to put a younger brother or sister through college.

Ultimate concern happens in friendships when, for example, one person refuses a better job offer which calls for moving to a different city rather than be separated from a friend.

In third-self friendship, ultimate concern calls forth the deepest expressions of love. Third-self friendship is synonymous with love. Paul the apostle's famous description of love gives an excellent summary of third-self friends and their ultimate concern for each other.

> Friends are patient and kind,
> they are not jealous or boastful,
> they are not arrogant or rude.
>
> Friends do not insist on their own way,
> they are not irritable or resentful,
> they do not rejoice at wrong,
> but delight in what is right.

Friendship bears all things,
believes all things,
hopes all things,
endures all things.

Friendship never ends (I Cor. 13:4–8).

Friendships among Artists

Friends for twenty-seven years, Spencer Tracy and Katharine Hepburn enjoyed both an acting partnership and a private relationship. "They influenced each other more than they realized," a biographer wrote. "They brought out the best in each other, in life, and in work." [12] They were artists at work; they were artists in their friendship.

So were poet Gertrude Stein and painter Pablo Picasso—although she disliked his art.

They met at a dinner party when she absentmindedly reached for a piece of bread, and he snatched it back yelling. She laughed at his possessiveness, he became embarrassed, and a third self began between them. Her biographer writes:

> For the next forty-one years, interrupted only by the quarrels that would inevitably result between two sensitive egos eager for acceptance and praise, they were to engage in friendly and familiar conversation. In Picasso's studio or at the rue de Fleurus, they would sit, knee to knee—Gertrude, large and formidable, in her chair; Picasso, small and intense in his—discussing the personal fortunes and habits of friends, the difficulties of their own work, their struggles, the state of the Parisian art world. Picasso had a fund of malicious observations about mutual acquaintances that Gertrude appreciated and remembered. He had, too, a way of summing up, in razor-sharp and emphatic statements, his ideas about art and the creative life that complemented and influenced her own way of thinking.[13]

12. Garson Kanin, *Tracy & Hepburn: An Intimate Memoir* (New York: Bantam Books, 1972), p. viii.
13. James R. Mellow, *The Charmed Circle: Gertrude Stein and Company* (New York: Praeger Publishers, 1974), p. 88.

In the Mind's Eye

Artists who constantly use their creative abilities learn to see in their mind's eye the "something they want to bring into existence." The something may be a triple somersault, a poem, a magazine-cover illustration or a third self of friendship.

Like any work of art, a third self needs to be creatively foreseen in the mind's eye. Such an interior vision may strongly influence growth in friendship.

Poet Robert Frost said, "Whenever I write a line, it is because that line has already been spoken clearly by a voice within my head, an audible voice." [14] He called himself poem-possessed.

Michelangelo, sculptor of the "Pieta," "Moses," "David," and many more famous works, could see in his mind's eye the work of art that lay buried in a piece of rock. "Every block of marble," explained Michelangelo in one of his sonnets, "holds within itself designs more beautiful than the greatest artist can conceive." [15]

According to Michelangelo, a sculptor then works to make real the rock's inner promise.

> Stroke by stroke, the practiced chisel brings out of the living rock its promise. And a form springs into life that can withstand time's rudest shocks.[16]

Friends are sculptors of their own lives.

As Michelangelo was able to see the artistic promise in a block of marble, people can learn to see with their inner vision the fullest potentials of third-self friendship.

14. Louis Mertins, *Robert Frost: Life and Talks—Walking* (Norman: University of Oklahoma Press, 1965), p. 197.
15. "Non Ha L'Ottimo Artista . . ." (1538/44).
16. "Se Ben Concetto . . ." (1545/46).

The Art of Friendship

While certain artists work more quickly than others, by letting the art emerge as they work, all artists display the requirements of discipline, concentration, patience and ultimate concern.

The reason some artists seem to work more quickly than others may be that they process the entire work of art in their heads beforehand, and that takes time.

Picasso painted rapidly, sometimes covering a large canvas in a day. When asked if a sketch he had made the day before was finished, he replied, "It would not be a finished canvas for Michelangelo, for instance, but it is for me."

His speed and intensity were possible because he thought out his creations in advance. Antonia Vallentin, one of his biographers, recalled Picasso pointing to his head and saying:

> Everything that happens is here. Before it reaches the end of the pen or the brush, the most important thing is to have it at one's fingertips, all of it, without losing anything.[17]

So too with friendship; the mind's eye and inner voice can creatively envision the form of close friendship or a third self. Third selves seldom happen without effort. Usually they come to life because friends envision the kind of friendship they want and are willing to become artists to bring it about.

There is an art of friendship and it can be learned. People can become artists at friendship. If they really want to, they find the time and energy to do it because of their ultimate concern.

17. Antonia Vallentin: *Picasso* (Garden City, N.Y.: Doubleday, 1963), pp. 10–11.

❧ 9 ❧

Stresses of Friendship

I never promised you a rose garden.
HANNAH GREEN

Friendship and Mental Health

Friendship brings out the best and worst in people.

It touches almost every feeling and emotion; it calls forth imagination, will power and action; it can challenge values, test ideas, nurture ideals.

Close friendship involves the total human being. It challenges the ability to form relationships that are deep and lasting. In friendship, people frequently demonstrate their emotional health or sickness.

Psychiatrist Theodore I. Rubin sometimes uses questions about friendship to test a patient's mental health. He feels there is usually strong hope for patients who have known long-lasting, satisfying friendships. He wrote:

> Long-term, happy friendships indicate that a person has a strong sense of self-worth, and the feelings and ability to give of himself or herself without fear of becoming depleted. People without friends are usually emotionally disturbed, withdrawn, and seclusive.[1]

1. Theodore I. Rubin, M.D., "Your Questions Answered," *Ladies Home Journal*, May 1975, p. 40.

Judy Garland's proverbial inability—or refusal—to communicate herself honestly prevented her from forming and keeping deep friendships. Her biographer Gerold Frank explained,

> The fact was that she did find it difficult to talk about herself. In many instances, it was too painful. In some, she was too ashamed. In others, she sought to maintain a mystery about herself, a reserve, a defense, so that people would not find out her vulnerable qualities and, with this knowledge, hurt her.[2]

When she did talk about herself, "Judy the entertainer" took over. She exaggerated, invented and twisted the facts. Over the years, she frequently changed her stories. "There is no doubt," wrote Gerold Frank, "that Judy Garland lived in her own special world of fantasy."

Friendship cannot be built on fantasy and daydreams. Making up stories about oneself may be exciting fun, but it does not serve well as the foundation of a lasting relationship. Such dream worlds exist "somewhere over the rainbow," but not on planet earth. Without clear communication, honest and direct, friendships may suffer heartbreaking stress.

The Stress of Silence

In friendship, many stresses begin because one or both friends will not talk about the relationship.

Sometimes, even friends who experience a third self find it difficult to speak openly about certain personal concerns.

Unhappy subjects seem most difficult to talk about. These may include personal physical illness, fear of losing a job, rejection by a spouse or anxiety about a child.

Paradoxically, some people even find it difficult to talk to a friend about personal good news. This may happen especially when the friend is unhappy. "How can I talk about landing my new job when Harry is out of work? I feel it would be like bragging, like hitting a guy when he's down."

2. Gerold Frank, *Judy* (New York: Harper & Row, 1975).

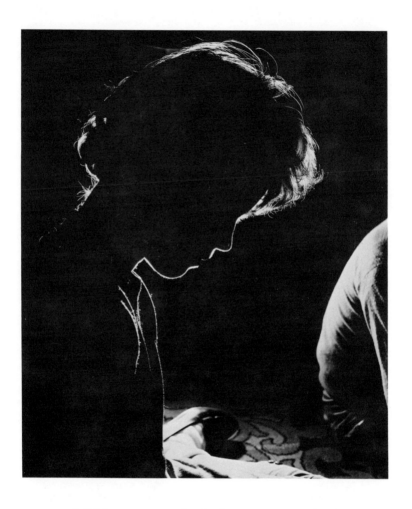

"Many stresses begin because one or both friends won't talk about their relationship"

Whether news is good or bad, certain people find excuses for not sharing it. They may be overflowing with strong feelings, yet they keep silent.

Sometimes, keeping quiet is not a bad idea. There can be a depth to silence that reaches beyond all words. But a third self may deteriorate if silence is often misunderstood.

The Fear of Talking

Friends who at times experience reluctance to talk about things important to the friendship sometimes are helped by talking about the *fear of talking*.

"I feel uncomfortable about discussing something," one might begin, "but I want to do it anyway. Okay?"

If *uncomfortable* isn't the precise feeling, they try other words like *ashamed, fearful, confused, anxious, afraid, upset* and so on. For example, "There is something that we need to talk about, and I'm afraid to do it but I think I must."

A statement like this opens up the topic. After a few anxious minutes, the friends may begin talking about the taboo subject as comfortably as they do about the weather.

Sometimes, even between friends who enjoy a pattern of openness, communication becomes difficult. Partners may signal such a communication snag by a comment like, "I'm really bothered by something, but I can't seem to talk about it."

When people say they *can't* talk, in reality they *won't*. According to Transactional Analysis, such unwillingness often relates to a Child form of rebellion disguised as helplessness.

Active listening can relieve communication snags. Acceptance without judgment often loosens the knot so that the words can flow smoothly and freely.

Once the flow begins, the active listening friend may respond with something like, "I'm glad you told me that." Then the pattern of openness begins again.

Some people feel stress if they talk about their loving feelings to each other.

They may want to express loving feelings but are afraid their friend cannot accept them. "If I ever told Ron that I liked him tremendously and that he was very special to me," said Ted, "he would be embarrassed out of his skin."

Others wish their friends would express loving feelings to them, but it never happens. "I know Gracie really likes me," explained Melissa, "and considers me her best friend—and I am—but I could wait till doomsday before she actually ever said it to me."

For many, talking about love is difficult. For others, listening to it is difficult.

People who want to describe their loving feelings often struggle to explain what they mean by the word "love." In the struggle to make clear and precise what they mean by "love," friends can clarify their relationship.

"Why did you do this for me?" Marylou asked Betty, her neighbor and close friend who had watched the children all afternoon while Marylou just took off for a few hours because she needed a break.

"Because I knew you'd do the same for me," replied Betty.

The two young mothers stood looking at each other. Their love for each other in friendship was strong, yet neither could find words to express it.

As Betty later explained, "When I can't express how I feel—and I know Marylou feels the same frustration—I may bring her a bunch of daisies, or find a card that says "I love you" and put it in the mail.

"I mean, we're basically in touch with each other. We each know, without saying, when the other would like a cup of tea, an ego-boost, or some help with the housecleaning.

"We talk about the intimate things in each other's lives," Betty continued. "We're completely at ease with each other, yet we feel frustrated in not being able to explain the emotions our relationship involves. So we end up just doing things for each other to show our love."

Love in friendship is often expressed *indirectly*, by words and action.

Astronaut John Glenn, who in 1962 was the first American to orbit the earth, had always been a man of action, not of words. From high school days, Annie Castor, his childhood sweetheart, wore a friendship ring John had given her. During college, he worked at the YMCA and saved for an engagement ring. Annie told the story this way.

> One night, about a month after Pearl Harbor, I didn't even notice for awhile that he'd slipped off my friendship ring and put this on. But here it is . . . I'm still wearing it.[3]

It seems that John never said a word about the engagement. "I don't remember a formal proposal from John," Annie said, "we both just knew."

Insatiable Friends

Some not-OK people expect too much of their friends. It seems they are not satisfied, no matter how many positive strokes they receive. They are insatiable.

Such people expect friends always to remember, always to be in a giving mood, to prefer their company to that of others, to understand and be sympathetic and never to hurt them or make mistakes. Expectations like these are impossible to fulfill and can stretch a friendship to the breaking point.

Actress Bette Davis, a strong personality, described such parasitic not-OK people as "weak." Bitterly, she wrote,

> The weak are the most treacherous of us all. They come to the strong and drain them. They are bottomless. They are insatiable. They are always parched and always bitter. They

3. Betty Garrett, "Annie and John Glenn: A Love Story," *McCall's*, March 1975, p. 28.

are everyone's concern and, like vampires, they suck our life's blood.

It is the strong who need care. It is they who need constant replenishment. It is the strong who are vulnerable. But, "Don't worry about her. She can take care of herself!" is what you hear from the beginning. It is the strong for whom I will do anything. It is they who need consideration.[4]

When people *do* get the positive attention they want or ask for, they should say so. For example, "I really like that from you" or "Just what I wanted" or "Thanks for that. It means a lot to me." Acknowledging a positive attention from a friend helps cement a relationship.

Disagreements and Differences

Though friends do not always *agree* with each other, as a rule they enjoy *understanding* each other. Sometimes voicing disagreements can help build mutual understanding.

Friends who golf together often also delight in arguing over their game. Musician friends enjoy playing music together, but also relish disputing over different interpretations of particular pieces of music. Co-workers cooperating in a project may enjoy working together, yet at times have divergent opinions on how to complete it.

To disagree is a privilege of friendship. Stendhal wrote: "There is nothing so delicious as the difference of decided opinions."

Friendships without differences are sometimes more limiting than freeing. Honest disagreements can be exciting and creative, when they are not used as putdowns but are designed to open further avenues of thought.

Disagreements, however, can put stress on a relationship. Certain common disagreements among friends are worth discussing.

4. Bette Davis, *The Lonely Life* (New York: G. P. Putnam, 1961), p. 222.

Inside and Outside Interests

Some people believe that friendship can exist only while friends share an outside interest or are involved together on a project. Friendship researchers feel that at least the *birth* of friendship seems directly related to some common interest or project.

By and large, common interests that spark friendship are "outside" interests, like baseball, stamp collecting, oil painting, dancing, high-fidelity equipment, nursing and volunteer work. However, a common interest of friends may also be an "inside" one, related to personal growth and psychological understanding. Some examples of "inside" interests may involve mutual encouragement in troubled times, listening to each other's problems and hopes, relaxation such as going to lunch together or meeting for coffee to break up a long day.

Once a close friendship, or a third self, develops, its focus may change from "outside" to "inside." In that case, the interpersonal relationship becomes centrally important, while the outside shared project takes a second place.

In special cases, where strong friendship has mellowed, the memory of what was, and enjoyment of what is, may be enough to keep the friendship alive.

New Needs

Sometimes disagreements occur among friends when one friend would like to involve new-needs levels in the friendship, but the other friend does not.

Imagine two friends who share an interest or a hobby such as photography. Then, as the relationship grows, one friend would like to introduce sexual involvement into it but the other does not. Here is a new need emerging in a relationship that should be talked about.

Many psychological games arise because people avoid talking about their feelings toward sexual involvement.

When the wish for sexual expression surfaces in a friendship, the friend who feels it should say so and why.

At the same time, he or she should be prepared for a "No," and consequent feelings of rejection. If the friendship is a true one, differences in feeling *can* be talked about, and often *need* to be.

Whether the attraction is heterosexual or homosexual, close friends should be open about their sexual feelings and needs. They should feel free enough to give or take a "No" as well as a "Yes."

When a friend would like to introduce new needs into a relationship—whether it be for security, belongingness, esteem, food, money or sexual expression—talking it out usually helps.

Samuel Clemens, better known to most people as Mark Twain, creator of *Huckleberry Finn*, once remarked how a new need could bring stress into a friendship.

> The holy passion of Friendship is so sweet and steady and loyal and enduring a nature that it will last through a whole lifetime, if not asked to lend money.

To begin a discussion about new needs, a friend might say, "I sense you'd like us to get involved at a new level. Is that right?" or "I sense you'd like to add something to our present relationship."

At this point, friends will usually listen to each other, sharing feelings, ideas and suggestions.

If one or another friend decides against the new need, he or she should say so. A typical statement of refusal might be, "I like you and our relationship is important to me. But I really don't want to move in that direction. It seems we have different needs."

Sometimes disagreements about needs lead to a new concern: the meaning of friendship in general.

It is important to clarify the meaning each gives to the word *friendship*. Friends may need to continue talking about the meaning of their relationship until each one's meaning for it is clear to both friends.

Unfortunately, in some cases, friends discover that their meanings are diametrically opposed, and that their relationship no longer makes sense. Usually, relationships like these return to a kind of casual friendship—which is better than becoming enemies, or playing games that generate nothing but frustration, fear, loneliness, jealousy and resentment.

Deep Feeling

Disagreements sometimes occur over deep feelings. As one person put it, "When my friend doesn't understand my deep feelings, I get very upset."

A lack of understanding between friends can occur for a number of reasons. First, one person may not understand the other because the feelings are being *experienced* but not clearly *communicated*. One cannot expect a friend always to "intuit" his or her feelings.

Second, the misunderstood person's feelings may relate to an experience that is unfamiliar to the other, or cannot be imagined by him or her. One who has not personally experienced jealousy or utter loneliness may not understand their significance in another person.

Third, misunderstanding may occur when the situations out of which the feelings arise have not been explained in a way that creates understanding. Listeners unfamiliar with the situation that contributed to the feelings may have a difficult time understanding them.

Fourth, friends may not want to understand another's deep feelings because they would find them too painful or too difficult to deal with.

Fifth, a simple explanation is sometimes that listeners are in fact preoccupied with their own feelings.

When friends feel a lack of understanding, it is important that they clarify the situation as soon as possible. In most cases, presuming the friendship is a close one, friends might say something like this:

"Hey, wait a minute. I don't feel as though you're understanding my feelings. May I explain again?"

Or, "I want to share my feelings with you. Please listen."

Or, "When you reject my feelings, I feel personally rejected."

Or, "Evidently you feel differently from me. I wonder if our needs are different at this moment, or if we're bringing some unfinished business into the situation."

Values Collisions

Sometimes disagreements are related to bigger issues, like personal values such as truth and love. When friends discover they have a values collision, the best approach is to admit it, to agree to disagree. After all, friends simply do not agree on everything.

Carol and Charles, a married couple who also enjoy a third-self friendship with each other, believe marriage does not demand total agreement. In fact, they disagree on many political issues.

"I think you're prejudiced," she says.

"I think you're naïve," he retorts.

By mutual agreement, they seldom discuss politics. "After all," she says, "why ruin a beautiful marriage because of political issues. These issues change from year to year, but our marriage is a permanent relationship."

Friendships That Weather Storms

Everyone knows that a house built on shifting sand is more likely to blow over in a hurricane than a house built on solid rock. The same is true of friendships. Well-founded relationships are better able to sustain stresses than superficial ones. Third-self friendships are best able to withstand even the strongest pressures and live through the storms.

Relationships that deal well with stresses seem to possess some or all of the following qualities:

The friends share a deep *commitment* to work things through.

They know *communications skills* for dealing with stresses.

They tend to be *flexible* and *tolerant* of each other's idio-syncrasies.

They *expect* important relationships to have some stress.

They are willing to restructure their *time* to deal with friend-ship crises.

They are basically *optimistic* about their relationship.

Detriments to Friendship

Why are there unfortunate and unhappy people who never have any friends at all? What are the qualities in such people that keep friendship from happening?

Personal qualities detrimental to friendship include envy, jeal-ousy and possessiveness. People who are domineering, over-solicitous, affection-hunters or psychological game players do not attract many close friends.

Many people, however, are already involved in relationships with such individuals and wonder how to deal with qualities in their friends that do not help the friendship to grow.

Jealousy and Dominance

Jealousy and possessiveness among friends are not uncom-mon. Many people want to be "first" with someone else.

The famous 1951 romance between baseball's "greatest living player" Joe DiMaggio and movie star Marilyn Monroe makes the point.

"DiMaggio had a strange pull on Marilyn," wrote a biographer. "He seemed to be the father she never knew—the strong silent man who encouraged her."

Their mutual attraction was obvious. Yet,

> Although he was generally loving and kind, DiMaggio was jealous of any attention Marilyn showed other men. He raised his voice to her on several such occasions. She reminded him gently that they were not married and pointed out that publicity was a vital part of her career.[5]

There was great ambivalence in his feelings toward her. Marilyn's press representative explained, "He wanted her for all the reasons any other man would want her, because she was a gorgeous woman, but didn't want her to be like that for any other man. It was an impossibility. He was a jealous man and couldn't accept her as a love object for every other man in the world."

If being "first" or "only" are serious problems in a relationship, it signals a symbiotic friendship. Jealous friends often feel incomplete without the other. For them, friendship turns half-people into wholes. Mathematically, they affirm,

$$\tfrac{1}{2} \text{ person} + \tfrac{1}{2} \text{ person} \rightarrow 1 \text{ person}$$

Psychologists say that the best way to elicit loyalty is to leave the other free. In many countries, slaves who are set free choose to remain with those whom they know and seemingly love.

Usually, envious friends find it difficult to let go, to let the other be free. Instead, they bind their friends; they are like masters who keep their slaves in chains.

Jealousy is often expressed in one friend acting overly solicitous or domineering over another. If in the domineering role, the simplest solution is to stop being judgmental. If in the submissive role, the simplest solution is to tell the friend to stop. Explain how their actions are interfering with the growth of friendship.

5. Maury Allen, *Where Have You Gone, Joe DiMaggio?* (New York: E. P. Dutton, 1975).

Admit negative feelings by saying something like: "I don't like it when anyone behaves with jealousy" or "I feel resentful around jealousy and want to withdraw."

Affection-Hunters

Some people have a need for affection that seems to be as deep as the Grand Canyon. Usually, they did not receive genuine affection as children. Affection-hunters are usually also possessive.

When you have friends who are affection-hunters, talk about it. Bring it into the open. Establish limits on how much of yourself you will share with them. Speaking to an insatiable affection-hunter, a friend might say, either verbally or nonverbally, "I will give you this much and no more. To give you more would be to deplete myself and would detract from the person I need to be."

To help themselves, affection-hunters may need to restructure their time. They might try finding more activities and involvements, or increasing the number of friends who will contribute to "filling up" the canyon.

The Stress of Pretense

When friends begin to pretend to each other, they begin to draw apart.

Pretense is a sign that a friendship is losing its vitality, perhaps dying. Little pretenses lead to bigger pretenses. The overall effect is destructive of true relationship.

Common pretenses include pretending interest when preoccupied with something or someone else, pretending approval when actually critical, pretending strength when feeling weak, pretending hope when feeling despair and vice versa.

Honesty does not mean telling somebody everything. It means being honestly who one is.

Frankness may include telling friends about their annoying personal habits. Those who care, do this gently.

First, they may ask for permission to express their feelings. For example, they say, "May I tell you something that's bothering me?" or "May I talk to you about something that really concerns me?" Or, "Would you be angry or hurt if I were to tell you something that I don't like?"

Faced with questions like these, spoken with genuine concern, people usually say Yes and are ready to listen less defensively than they would if criticized directly.

Sometimes it helps to describe the situation and the feelings it generates in "I" language, that is, the criticizer needs to "own" his or her own feelings about the friend's bad habits. Possible "I" statements might be "I feel *discounted* when you ignore me at a party" or "I feel *angry* if you call me only when you want to complain" or "I feel *disgust* when you chew your food and talk at the same time" or "I feel *turned off* when you continually talk of your interests and forget about mine."

In each example the criticizer "owns" a feeling.

After clearly stating their feelings about a friend's habits, they may sit back and *listen actively*.[6]

Misusing Friendship

One of the most blatant misuses of friendship is to buy and sell it. Rollo May observed,

> One of the chief things which keeps us from learning to love in our society is our "marketplace orientation." We use love for buying and selling. One illustration of this is in the fact that many parents expect that the child love them as a repayment for their taking care of him. To be sure, a child will learn to pretend to certain acts of love if the parents insist on

6. Basic communication skills such as "I" messages and active listening are described in any of Thomas E. Gordon's communication books, including *Parent Effectiveness Training* or *Teacher Effectiveness Training*, Peter Weyden, New York. For practice exercises, see Louis M. Savary, Mary S. Paolini, and George Lane *Interpersonal Communication*, Loyola University Press, Chicago, 1975.

it; but sooner or later it turns out that a love demanded as a payment is no love at all.[7]

And so with friendship. Whenever it is purchased with gifts or forced upon someone by pressures or threats, it is not friendship at all.

Almost equally difficult to deal with are those who misuse compliments or praise as a means of acquiring friends. A simple word for this is flattery. Flattery is in direct opposition to a well-deserved compliment or a positive stroke, for two reasons: first, flattery usually comes from a person who is neurotic and not-OK; second, its goal is usually a form of symbiotic attachment. As a result, friendships founded on flattery are likely to go nowhere fast.

Eileen Guder summed it up.

> I know that many of us, in our longing for friendship, do try to earn it by an inordinate attempt to please, by flattery, sometimes by toadying; but that is a sick sort of approach, born out of our inner uncertainties about our own worth as a friend.[8]

Custom in modern society approves and even encourages empty flattery. Those who find themselves being seduced into this phony way of relating can become aware of it and guard against it.

Finally, there is a third way of misusing friendship that causes stress in relating. It is used by people who really don't want to relate at all. Many people who say they want friends really just want a shoulder to cry on, someone to fight their battles or an escort to parties. They are not concerned with the relationship itself but with using the other person to carry out their plans.

Such people are not interested in forming a third self. "My self" is the only self that concerns them.

---

7. Rollo May, *Man's Search for Himself* (New York: W. W. Norton, Signet ed., 1953), p. 208.
8. Eileen Guder, *The Many Faces of Friendship* (Waco, Texas: Word Books, 1969), p. 29.

Sometimes, such people may be unaware of their motivation.

"I want to be friends with you," said a thirty-year-old student to her teacher, also a woman. "I have so much to learn from you."

"But what would we be friends about?" asked the teacher. "From what I hear you saying now, our friendship would be be built only on my telling you what I know and you taking it all in. That's not enough for me."

People may experience stress in relating when they have different expectancies and priorities, or when they do not live up to the ones they have verbally or nonverbally agreed upon.

Exclusive Friends

What happens when friends become so preoccupied with each other that they exclude the rest of the world?

Ignace Lepp described a pair of exclusive friends as "the narcissistic we." Such couples are usually so enamored of each other that they see nothing and no one else besides themselves. They are themselves as halves of a whole.

Rita, a young divorcée, described a narcissistic "we" she had experienced with her former husband. "When we were married three years ago, Stan and I were so totally enamored with each other that we felt perfectly complete as humans. We saw less and less of our friends. We made excuses not to see them even when they insisted. Pretty soon we were alone together. It was deliciously enjoyable for awhile. Then, all of a sudden, one day Stan said to me, 'I've had it. Goodbye.' And he left. Sitting there I realized I had made no contact with friends, other than Stan, in almost two years."

This kind of preoccupation puts a burden on friends to satisfy each other's needs and desires totally. Narcissistic "we's" also place a stress on other friends who would like to relate to the exclusive couple.

Exclusive friendships occur when the friendship focuses attention totally on the relationship. Sometimes mere mutual fascination is enough to initiate a narcissistic "we." At other times, the couple decide that their relationship is so important that it is worth working on to the exclusion of others.

Frank and Bob were always seen together. They ate, worked and went to films together. When only one of them was invited somewhere, they refused the invitation. "It's both of us or neither of us," they seemed to say. Slowly, one by one, other long-standing friendships died. "We don't want to spread ourselves thin," they said. "We are first priority for each other."

Those outside the friendship who liked Frank or Bob felt "left out." But there was not much they could do.

The Stress of Sharing Friends

Other problems occur when people begin to share their friends.

Some people may want all their third selves to be the same. "He's not like my other good friends," a person might think, "so something must be wrong."

People naturally compare relationships, but to demand that all relationships be of the same mold can destroy the uniqueness of each. Friends are not all alike. They are not stamped out by a cookie cutter on an assembly line. Besides, a steady diet of the same kind of cookies becomes boring.

To get the most out of a relationship, those involved need to focus on its uniqueness, its special pattern of needs and personality. It is more exciting to have many different kinds of flowers in a garden than to have everything the same.

The point is that no friendship can be like any other, even if on the surface they appear alike. In a bed of American Beauty roses, each rose will be seen to be unique if you just look closely enough.

When people are telling friends of their love for other friends, it is important to remind them that loving others does not lessen love for them. Let friends know that other close relationships enrich all of a person's relationships. Let friends also know that it's all right if they love others, too.

As long as friendship is freely given and freely received, its love is unconditional and tends to spread outward to others. Love usually can multiply without losing its intensity.

As long as friendship is unconditional, as long as friends can say, "I love you no matter what," their relationship will remain free of psychological games.

Growing Out of a Friendship

Another friendship problem occurs when one friend grows and matures faster than another.

One person put it this way: "As far as Marge is concerned, our friendship is still where it was five years ago. And I've grown a lot since then. I wish our relationship had evolved too."

In cases like these, a "fast-growing" friend may sometimes become impatient and want the relationship to change in line with her growth. One of the best things for a "growing" friend to do is to love the friend for what she is right now. Within a few months, Marge might experience a growth spurt and surpass her "growing" friend.

Remember, too, that people as a rule tend to resist change. They may sense some risk and be unwilling to take a chance. Besides, old ways of growth, though slow, are familiar and predictable and seem somehow safer than new ways.

Psychologists sometimes suggest that friends discuss the lack of growth in their relationship. Like fertilizer, honest discussions may stimulate new growth.

Stress in Marriage

Spouses are sometimes each other's best friends but often they are enemies. When husbands and wives lose their friendship, it is usually very painful. They try to diagnose the pain.

Sometimes they conclude a friendship never existed in the first place!

Sometimes they conclude that, if there had been a friendship once upon a time and it is now disintegrating, it never would have developed into a genuine third self anyway.

Frequently spouses discover that for years they merely enjoyed a mutual need-filling relationship. Through their married years, they have been "servicing" each other's physical and security needs without growing together into other areas in which a third self might have developed.

As Emily Coleman put it:

> Many marriages and other close relationships are terminated by a woman who gets sick and tired of being worked for, instead of being paid attention to.[9]

Many men get sick and tired of the same thing.

Even when spouses have enjoyed a third self, it may die for many reasons. In some cases, the Adult ego state of each has expanded with new information, ideas or interests which they have not shared with each other and they end up with little in common. In other cases, priorities have shifted so that a job, a house, a hobby or children may be consuming almost all of one's time and energy so that little of either is left for the spouse.

In each of these cases, dialogue between spouses and reassessment of their relationship seems necessary. Couples may need a few visits with a marriage counselor. Just as people visit a dentist annually for a check-up, couples can visit a counselor for a marriage check-up.

In some cases, couples have built up so much resentment that it seems impossible to recover the warmth and caring that they knew in the beginning. Certain couples find that a

9. Emily Coleman, *Making Friends with the Opposite Sex* (Los Angeles: Nash, 1972), p. 163.

reasonable goal is a "friendly divorce" which will not scar them or their children any more than necessary.

Katharine Hepburn, Spencer Tracy and Louise Tracy, his wife, had an open relationship.

Once when Kate and Spencer were on their way to a private picnic at Malibu, Spencer collapsed with severe chest pains. A rescue squad rushed him to St. Vincent's Hospital.

> Kate, acting with her customary sweetness of character, also called Mrs. Tracy immediately. The two women kept alternate vigils by Tracy's bedside until, his sickness diagnosed as a temporary congestion of the respiratory tract, he was released, with Louise Tracy's approval, to Kate's care.[10]

A few years later Spencer became ill again and had to be hospitalized. Once again Kate and Mrs. Tracy kept vigil in alternating day and night shifts for six weeks. Each day they wrote notes on the patient's progress for each other when they changed shifts.

During the months of recovery, Kate would visit him at his home and together they would go for long walks in the Hollywood hills. The relationship could handle stress.

Many married people who enjoy close relationships with others, either same-sex or opposite-sex friendships, find it difficult to talk to spouses about them.

If the marriage is built upon trust, openness and commitment, they need only initiate talk about extra-marital friendships. Then their third self will usually deal lovingly with it.

However, where marriages are shaky, or if spouses are possessive or threatened by outside involvement, then spouses with outside friends may need to think twice before talking about them. They might first ask themselves, "Why do I want to talk to my spouse about this?" or "How might this information affect my spouse?" or "Am I merely looking for permis-

10. Charles Higham, *Kate: The Life of Katharine Hepburn* (New York: W. W. Norton, 1975).

sion from my spouse to have other relationships?" or "Am I looking for approval?" or "Am I seeking acceptance because I feel guilty about my friend?" or "Do I want my spouse to forbid me and restrict me from outside relationships?" or "Am I trying to generate jealousy?" or "Would I like to prove that someone else thinks I'm important?"

In a word, such spouses may ask themselves *why* they want to talk about outside friendships before they do it. Perhaps they will decide not to do it.

Three-Person Friendships

Any group can be the matrix for several third-self friendships if the situation is treated with delicacy.

Three-person friendships are very special situations. Growth will happen if those involved don't push or force, if they don't insist or presume.

Simone de Beauvoir's statement, "Respect each other's privacy and deal gently with each other's dreams" is very sound advice for three-or-more-person friendships.

Game-playing is easy to do in a group of three and it's dangerous. Usually, games align two against one. The object of such games is to pair off with one person and reject the third. Three-person friendships are difficult to sustain among insecure, jealous or domineering people.

Pianist Johannes Brahms with Robert and Clara Schumann, three affectionate and highly emotional people, also enjoyed a close three-person friendship, though Brahms suffered inner storms and stress for awhile.

Robert and Clara took the fair-haired, twenty-year-old Brahms into their home and into their friendship. Almost too quickly, Brahms learned to love Clara Schumann, fourteen years his senior and mother of seven children. This made him feel guilty because he also loved and revered her husband, Robert, as his "friend and benefactor, above all others."

After Robert's death, Brahms's relationship with Clara slowly evolved into a deep lifelong friendship. Twenty years later he could still write to her. "I love you more than myself and more than anybody and anything on earth."

Toward the end of his life, when the forty-year-old relationship was almost broken because of a misunderstanding, he wrote to Clara,

> Today you must allow me to repeat to you that you and your husband represent the most beautiful experience of my life, that you stand for its greatest wealth and noblest meaning.[11]

Ideally, in a three-person relationship there can be four "third selves"—three-friendship pairs, and a third self made up of all three friends. Any combination of third selves is possible.

As long as the three people involved do not feel threatened, they can allow for the fact that the strength and prominence of each of these four third selves may wax and wane at different times.

At one moment Tom and Dick may be closely involved, at another it may be Dick and Harry. And at some moments, all three may be close and together.

Too Many Friends?

According to Charlie Brown, nobody can have too many friends. "I need all the friends I can get," says he.

Other thinkers, referred to earlier, recommend only one or two close friends. Each one needs to answer this question for himself.

Probably the demands and expectations of friendship will determine how many close friends a person has time and energy for.

11. Joseph Machlis, *The Enjoyment of Music* (New York: W. W. Norton, 1963), pp. 178–179.

❧ *"I need all the friends I can get"*

Futurologist Robert Theobald suggests that in coming years people's need to travel will lessen because:

> *we will not want to leave our friends*, and because we will have the technological capacity to create varying environments within a given community. The technology will be ready when we have decided what we want.[12]

12. Robert Theobald, *An Alternative Future for America II* (Chicago: Swallow, 1970), p. 45.

✺ 10 ✺

Communities of Friendship

Because of friendship, we see with different eyes
not only our own lives but the entire universe.
IGNACE LEPP

The Age of Aquarius

Sometime around 1970, the Age of Aquarius arrived on planet
earth.

Young people began looking at the universe with new eyes and
hearing its message with new ears. In the minds of American
youth, rock music became the symbol for a new consciousness.

"To us, rock music represents freedom," wrote youth prophet
Alan Oken, "the freedom to feel, to be one, with a higher
collective force, to move together in one cosmic rhythm." [1]

"It gave a person the sensation of being oneself *and more than
oneself* at the same time," explained another young man.

Caught up in the irresistible beat of rock, young people felt
a common unity with each other. Because their music bridged
ideologies and personal differences, it seemed to them a uni-
fying love force in the world.

When Beatles drummer Ringo Starr sang, "I get by with a
little help from my friends," everybody under thirty years

1. Alan Oken, "The Age of Aquarius," © 1970 by Alan Oken.

old flashed on the implications. Ringo was singing the praises of a worldwide friendship community for young people.

Youthful thinker Martin Jezer explained how this universal community revolved around friendship.

> We had our friends, or we had nothing. And our friends became our family, and these families became a tribe, and when half a million of us surfaced at Woodstock, we realized we had become a Nation.[2]

Abbie Hoffman called them "Woodstock Nation."

Because of impossibly oppressive social and cultural pressures, Woodstock Nation and most of the hippie love communes that were scattered around the world slowly disappeared. But the idea behind them didn't.

Friendship Communities

The idea of friendship communities has always been attractive.

In ancient Greece, Socrates was the center of an almost inseparable group of friends. In fact, friendship figured so strongly in Socrates' thought that he set himself to teach and to practice the art of acquiring friends.

Plato and Aristotle also attracted their disciples more as friends than as students.

In Palestine, Jesus began a group of friends who eventually would go out into every corner of the world proclaiming a message of cosmic friendship, a universal attitude of love toward all humanity.

"The whole body of believers was united in heart and soul," records the writer of the Acts of the Apostles. "Not a man of them claimed any of his possessions as his own, but everything was held in common. . . . it was distributed to anyone who stood in need" (Acts 4:32–35).

2. Martin Jezer, "Family, Tribe and the Quest for Community," © 1970 by Martin Jezer.

Paul, one of Jesus' apostles, viewed all humanity as one body and one spirit. He traveled ceaselessly, spending all his energy in developing and nourishing Christian love communities.

Among the many Christian friendship communities, the Jesuits are an outstanding example. Founded by Ignatius Loyola in the sixteenth century, their community began as a group of friends studying together at the University of Paris. From the first, they called themselves the Friends of Jesus, and vowed to maintain their closeness and friendship to each other, no matter where their work called them. Indissoluble friendship remains a characteristic of modern-day Jesuits.

The urge for friendship-unity is not limited to certain places in the world.

Burma-born Buddhist Secretary-General of the United Nations U Thant, a humble man, was a friend to all. He viewed the giant assembly as a common instrument for dealing with the challenges of world peace and justice. His Buddhist training and his education in the West led him to view all humanity as a potential community of friends. His work at the United Nations involved building friendship. Shortly before his death he wrote in his journal,

> I wake up in the morning as a Buddhist and a Burmese and meditate at least for a short while in order to set my work, actions and thoughts into the right perspective. . . .

> But when I enter my office in Manhattan, you will understand that I must forget that I am a Burmese and a Buddhist. One of my duties is to receive many people. . . . In order to receive and fully understand what my human brother has to say to me, I open myself to him, I must empty myself of myself.[3]

Three Driving Desires

In 1859 in a small village in Russia's Ukraine, Sholom Rabino-

3. Quoted in "U Thant Passes Away," *New Age Journal,* 1:3 (February 1975), p. 11.

witz was born. He was part of the Jewish community in exile there.

Some people will remember him by his pen name, Sholom Aleichem. As a prolific Yiddish folk writer, a Jewish Mark Twain, his stories fill over twenty-eight volumes.

Many more will smile with recognition at Aleichem's famous character, Tevye the Dairyman, whom they saw in the Broadway musical and screenplay, *Fiddler on the Roof*.

Sholom Aleichem had three driving desires in life. All three were part of his design to help create a friendship community among his fellow Jews in exile.

First, he wanted to raise the artistic tastes of his Yiddish-speaking people—so he wrote classically beautiful but simple stories that everyone would read. They have become a chronicle for posterity.

Second, he wanted to help strengthen the collective consciousness of his Jewish friends—so he wrote stories about Jewish people, their deepest roots, and the biblical tradition. Tevye, always slightly misquoting the Bible, overflows with a sense of his community as "the chosen people."

Third, Aleichem wanted to bring laughter to the faces of his people in exile—so he wrote stories that made people laugh. He once wrote in a letter,

> The world is in a miserable state, and just on spite we ought not to cry about it. And, if you want to know the truth, that's the source of my perpetually good mood, my humor. Just on spite, I'm not going to cry. Just to spite them, there's going to be laughter.[4]

He expressed awareness of community among the Jewish people. He strengthened their potential for collective friendship.

---

4. Sholom Aleichem, *Old Country Tales*, ed. and intro. by Curt Leviant (New York: G. P. Putnam, 1966), p. 14.

Once a Jew came up to Sholom Aleichem in Warsaw, took his hand and kissed it, saying, "You are our consolation. You have sweetened for us the bitterness of exile." [5]

The Influence of Friendship Groups

Impelled by love for humanity and the desire for unity, groups of people have always felt urged to come together in friendship.

The Quakers, or Friends, as they prefer to be called, were founded about 1650 under the leadership of George Fox. For centuries, Quaker friendship bonds withstood continual persecution in Europe as well as in America.

The Friends were characterized by a concern for social needs. Their energies helped prison reform, they campaigned against slavery, urged justice for the American Indian, and supported humane treatment of insane persons. They vigorously opposed war, and were first to organize relief systems for war refugees.

Despite their small numbers, Quakers have been extremely effective in helping make the world a more peaceful place. Their effectiveness probably stems from their dedication to friendship and their desire to bring about a world of friends.

In contrast to the hopefulness of the Friends, certain people discount the possibility of world-wide friendship. To these, paleontologist and evolutionary theologian Pierre Teilhard de Chardin once remarked,

> If, as you claim, a universal love is impossible, how can we account for that irresistible instinct in our hearts which leads us toward unity whenever and in whatever our deepest emotions are stirred. A universal love is not only psychologically possible, it is the only complete and final way in which we are able to love.[6]

5. *Ibid.*, p. 19.
6. See Pierre Teilhard de Chardin, *Human Energy* (New York: Harcourt, Brace, Jovanovich, 1969), pp. 82–84.

≈§ "*Impelled by love for humanity and the desire for unity, groups of people have always felt urged to come together in friendship*"

Friendship Founded on Bodies

Friendship is usually recognized as a kind of spiritual communion. However, since humans are not pure spirits, friendships need to be founded on bodies as well as on minds or spirits.

If worldwide friendship is ever to become a reality on earth, the needs of bodies must first be cared for. As someone once remarked, "It's pretty hard to be concerned about friendship with the whole world when I'm hungry, sick, tired, or frightened."

Jane Addams recognized the needs of human bodies. She was a wonder to all who knew her, and a friend to people infected by ignorance and poverty.

In the southwest district of Chicago, Jane saw all nationalities thrown together in a community living in squalor and filth. Here she founded Hull House. Gradually overcoming the distrust of her neighbors, she invited people to her settlement and organized clubs, societies, homes and classes for them.

Solving the problems of her own neighborhood gave her the hope that America, through the spread of her ideals, would adopt her approach to better understanding among people. In fact, Hull House came to be known all over the world.

Working toward a better way of life for those who suffered in poverty or trouble was Jane Addams's way of life—really, her religion.

An old Chicago workman once said of her, "Her no just one people. Her no just one religion. Her all people, all religions."

Concern for the Forgotten

On the opposite end of the social ladder, but still very much concerned with needs of the body, stands Russian-born Anna Pavlova, one of the world's greatest ballerinas. Her favorite flower was the forgotten violet. And that symbolized her warm and vital concern for "forgotten" people.

"Anna Pavlova never had children of her own," wrote her friend Sol Hurok, "but it was to youngsters that she was most vulnerable." [7]

For decades in Paris, she maintained a home for about thirty Russian refugee children.

Wherever she performed, she watched over the girls in her dance company. Like an older friend, she felt personally responsible for their welfare. At holidays or birthdays, each ballerina received a carefully chosen present.

And she never forgot her old ballet friends in Russia. For many years after she left her homeland, Anna used to send relief packages from America to ballerinas from the Bolshoi and Maryinsky theaters.

In these ways, she kept alive friendship bonds with many people in different places.

Representative Friends

"What happens to the person's own body," wrote theologian Jean Danielou, "is identical with what happens in the universe." [8]

The bodies of certain individuals come to represent many other humans. One special person stands for a multitude of people.

One such important "representative friend" was John L. Lewis, giant of the American labor movement. His body and voice, sometimes gruff and thundering, symbolized the great strengths and weaknesses of American workers.

One thing everyone knew for sure, especially public officials, was that John L. Lewis was dedicated to working people. He was their friend and would go to any lengths to maintain their rights.

7. Sol Hurok, "My Most Unforgettable Character—Anna Pavlova," *Reader's Digest*, February 1968, p. 74.
8. Jean Danielou, *Lord of History* (Chicago: Henry Regnery, 1958), p. 191.

One instance occurred when Lewis went to Flint, Michigan, in 1937 to defend his workers' sit-down strike at the General Motors Plant there.

Michigan Governor Frank Murphy was about to declare a state of insurrection and order the National Guard to evict the workers. Murphy showed his insurrection order to Lewis, hoping Lewis would relent in the face of the National Guard.

Mr. Lewis refused. So late at night in Lewis's hotel room Governor Murphy asked him what he would do if the Guard were called out to the GM plant the next morning.

Following a suitable pause, Lewis replied:

> You want my answer, sir? I give it to you. Tomorrow morning, I shall personally enter General Motors plant Chevrolet No. 4. I shall order the men to disregard your order.
>
> I shall then walk up to the largest window in the plant, open it, divest myself of my outer raiment, remove my shirt and bare my bosom. Then, when you order your troops to fire, mine will be the first breast those bullets will strike.
>
> And as my body falls from that window to the ground, you listen to the voice of your grandfather [he had been hanged in Ireland by the British for rebellion] as he whispers in your ear, "Frank, are you sure you're doing the right thing?" [9]

The Governor was reported turning pale, his body quivering, as he left the room. The order was never issued. Next day General Motors capitulated, and, once again, John L. Lewis had been a faithful friend to the workingmen.

Brothers with Community Concern

Third-self friendship that springs up among family members sometimes spreads outward toward concern.

The Wright brothers, Wilbur and Orville, were friends from boyhood in Dayton, Ohio. In mutual friendship, they worked

9. Alden Whitman, *The Obituary Book* (New York: Stein & Day, 1971), pp. 190–191.

together to develop the fundamental principles of aerodynamics. As their gift to the human race, they introduced people to air travel, facilitating contact between members of the one body of humanity.

The Mayo brothers, Dr. William and Dr. Charles, were inseparable medical geniuses. Together they developed many revolutionary surgical techniques. Their love for each other spilled over into concern for the sick. Inspired by these brothers, the Sisters of St. Francis promised to build a hospital for their surgical experiments and staff it with nurses. Today, as a memorial to these men, their hospital in Rochester, Minnesota, is called the Mayo Clinic.

Ever-Widening Circles

People who can open themselves to embrace the concerns and needs of many other people are indeed beautiful people.

Friendship coaxes such beautiful people out of hiding. It also encourages their power to act.

According to Maslow's hierarchy of needs, all-inclusive love and unity are activated on the self-actualizing level of growth.

The more people act, the more they permit their inner potentials to be actualized. When they act in friendship, in a third self, their potentials seem to increase even more.

Friendship seems to release unsuspected powers in the inner core.

The power unleased in friendship reaches out in ever-widening circles of influence. This power takes on various forms.

In New York in 1891, composer and conductor Walter Damrosch reorganized the Symphony Orchestra and inaugurated a series of concerts for children, as well as Sunday concerts for the general public.

During the first years of radio, in 1925, he conducted the first symphony concert radio broadcast.

In 1929, as musical director of NBC, he began its Music Appreciation Course, which reached six million American school children and three million adult listeners.[10]

Damrosch was energized by music. It symbolized for him the link between himself and millions of potential friends.

Those Who Bear the Mark of Pain

The urge for universal friendship emerged in Navy medical officer Dr. Tom Dooley. It surfaced in his power to heal people.

For years, Dooley and hundreds of concerned friends worked under primitive conditions in southeast Asian jungle hospitals.

Dooley's volunteers called themselves the Fellowship of Those Who Bear the Mark of Pain. As the group grew, it became a universal friendship community, as Dooley explained.

> I and my men have found this Fellowship wherever we have gone. Who are its members? Dr. Albert Schweitzer believes the members are those who have learned by experience what physical pain and bodily anguish mean. These people, all over the world, are united by a secret bond.

> He who has been delivered from pain must not think he is now free, at liberty to continue his life and forget his sickness. He is a man whose eyes are opened. He now has a duty to help others in their battles with pain and anguish. He must help to bring to others the deliverance which he himself knows.[11]

Members of this fellowship included not only those who were formerly sick, but also those who were related to sufferers. Obviously, it was an all-embracing fellowship.

In acting with and for each other, they gained access to a higher level of awareness and action which they would never

---

10. Noel Ames, *These Wonderful People: Intimate Moments in Their Lives* (Chicago: Peoples Book Club, 1947), p. 35.
11. Thomas A. Dooley, M.D., *The Edge of Tomorrow* (New York: Farrar, Straus and Cudahy, 1961), Foreword.

have attempted alone. They achieved their success by sharing the power within their inner cores.

The Medicine of Laughter

Energy for universal brotherhood may surface anywhere. The pull of cosmic friendship can evoke responses from the most unsuspecting places.

As a child, comedian Danny Kaye always wanted to be a physician. "When I was young," he said, "I wanted to be a doctor because the idea of making people happy appealed to me."

Instead, for the past twenty years, since UNICEF first asked him for help, he has been bringing the medicine of laughter to children all over Europe and Asia.

From Istanbul to Bangkok, with grinning face, shaggy red hair, and battered golf hat, Danny has been an ambassador of friendship to the world. And mirth has been his universal language.

> I just try to make people laugh. I play to kids who have never heard of America, much less Danny Kaye.
>
> It's the most wonderful thing I have ever done.
>
> If we can better understand the problems of the world's children, the world might be well on its way to understanding itself.[12]

A Clear Invitation

Invitations to universal friendship may also surface in simple ways, for example, through a poem, a book or a song. Sometimes the simplest invitations, because they are genuine, have profound effects on people.

In March of 1948, a copy of Nat King Cole's recording of the song "Nature Boy" was delivered to music librarian Al Trilling

12. John Reddy, "Danny Kaye: Pied Piper of Laughter," *The Kiwanis Magazine,* November 1974.

at radio station WNEW in New York City. He played it through once and rushed it directly to a disc jockey.

"It's one of the most beautiful songs ever written. It's almost a tone poem," Trilling explained. "The words and music answer the longing in everyone's heart."

After every performance of "Nature Boy" on the air, the station would get twenty-five or thirty phone calls.

People heard the closing line of the haunting melody—"the greatest thing you'll ever learn is just to love, and be loved in return"—as the answer to the war-weary world's need for peace and friendship.

A clear invitation to universal friendship, the song had been written and left at Nat King Cole's office by an unknown composer, Eden Ahbez.

Cole's staff reported the man as having long hair, wearing sweat shirt, dungarees, and sandals. Later it was discovered that he was a practicing yogi, who lived out of a sleeping bag somewhere in the Hollywood Hills. Cole's manager said he found Ahbez meditating under one of the L's in the big HOLLYWOOD sign on the hillside. "Nature Boy" had burst forth from his heart's deepest core.

The song went on to become an all-time favorite. People who were alive in 1948 still remember the song, not because it is cute or clever, but because "the words and music answer the longing in everyone's heart."[13]

"The greatest thing you'll ever learn is just to love, and be loved in return."

Universal Friends

"Love is not primarily a relationship to a specific person," explained psychologist Erich Fromm. "It is an attitude, an

13. Maria Cole with Louie Robinson, *Nat King Cole: An Intimate Biography* (New York: William Morrow, 1971), pp. 30–33.

*"The greatest thing you'll ever learn is
just to love and be loved in return"*

orientation of character which determines the relatedness of a person to the world as a whole." [14]

Friendship cannot remain locked up with one individual. Of its nature, its love is open to others and welcomes them into its friendship. Fromm writes,

> If I truly love one person, I love all persons, I love the world, I love life. If I can say to somebody else, "I love you," I must be able to say, "I love you in everybody, I love through you the world, I love in you also myself." [15]

The call of cosmic friendship, as Teilhard de Chardin described it, is "an irresistible instinct in our hearts."

But to really experience this universal love, explained K. von Durckheim, "One must break through to the world where all things are essentially one body." [16]

Certain charismatic individuals, like Abraham Lincoln, Dag Hammarskjöld, Martin Luther King, Jr., and Gandhi, symbolized this one body. They somehow seemed to unify in themselves a whole world of people.

In such leaders, myriad people are made to feel the unity of one body, without losing their individual identities and importance.

Many American families considered President John F. Kennedy an inspiring friend. "Ask not what your country can do for you but what you can do for your country," he said in his inaugural address. He was clearly calling the American people to national unity. Many responded to the invitation.

Symbolic individuals often evoke friendship bonds with millions of people.

14. Erich Fromm, *The Art of Loving* (New York: Harper & Row, 1956). See "The Objects of Love," pp. 38–39. (Bantam ed.)
15. *Ibid.*
16. K. von Durckheim, *The Japanese Cult of Tranquility* (London, 1960), p. 83.

Gandhi was such a charismatic individual. He seemed to be a universal friend. Thousands, even millions, of men and women considered themselves friends of Gandhi. Many who never met him, or were not alive while he was, unhesitatingly called him friend.

On Gandhi's death, Leon Blum, a former French premier, wrote,

> I never saw Gandhi. I do not know his language. I never set foot in his country, and yet I feel the same sorrow as if I had lost someone near and dear. The whole world has been plunged into mourning by the death of this extraordinary man.[17]

Gateway to Universal Friendship

Third-self friendship can be a gateway to universal friendship. This is a further development.

However, to see universal friendship as a possibility, people need to experience, with one person at least, a direct communion. This involves a sharing of everything personal, not merely ideas and possessions.

Ignace Lepp claims that

> . . . as long as we have not lived the experience of a solid and deep friendship we can only have a pessimistic vision of human nature.[18]

At best, friendless people live on the fringe of existence. They know little of friendship's shared life. They have not swum in the continually intensifying river of coexistence, called the third self. They have not entered the "between-ness" that can transcend time and space.

Helicopter pilot Lon Spurdock experienced direct communion

17. Louis Fischer, *Gandhi: His Life and Message for the World* (New York: New American Library, 1954), p. 7.
18. Ignace Lepp, *The Ways of Friendship* (New York: Macmillan, 1966), p. 113.

with his wife even on rescue missions over Vietnam battle-grounds. In a letter to his wife, he wrote:

> My love for you is always with me—in the helicopter, in the swamps, in the ambush—and I feel it especiallly strong when the bullets zip and crack and hiss and thud nearby. It strength-ens me, gives me confidence, and always stands as a reason for pressing on when things look grim. . . .
>
> You are my foundation, my source of strength, my hope, my best friend, my only value, and my only concrete reason for living. On the fringe of existence—and I have been there—everything else disappears.[19]

Only gradually do friends acquire the unshakable certainty in their friendship that Lon Spurdock and his wife knew.

The Spurdocks learned to realize, in Lepp's words, "that they are not two solitudes chance has brought together but that the same spiritual sap circulates in them." [20]

Sometimes, when people are overeager to become close friends, they react impatiently to the process. Like children, they may wish to eliminate it entirely. To expect an intense friendship to be made as quickly as a cup of instant coffee only shows ignorance of what growth in friendship is all about.

No Reason to Stop

It would be nice if tomorrow morning everyone on earth was able to be truly a friend to all other human beings.

For the moment, and probably for a long time to come, most humans will still feel too restricted to embrace and welcome truly universal friendship.

Few people seem to be able to approach even a quasi-cosmic friendship.

19. Quoted in *Learning to Feel—Feeling to Learn* by Harold C. Lyon, Jr. (Columbus, Ohio: Charles E. Merrill, 1971), pp. x–xi.
20. Ignace Lepp, *The Ways of Friendship*, p. 115.

But this is no reason for people to stop wanting to form a worldwide community.

Nor is it reason for people to stop forming ever-widening circles of friends and communities.

Sometimes two people claim to find total fulfillment in each other. "We need no one else," they might say. But psychologists ask such intimates to think twice and look around.

According to Robert Theobald, it seems unrealistic to expect two people completely to satisfy each other's need for a full, ever-developing life.

> The idea that one can find everything that one needs in one other person, without other close relationships, is a tragic distortion of the meaning of community. We need to develop a very wide range of diverse communities.[21]

Just as friendship can increase people's power for action, it is in and through action that people strengthen their capacity for love and for community.

Cosmic Friendship

Cosmic friendship seems to be an evolutionary stage that our planet has yet to achieve.

Teilhard de Chardin viewed the history of the universe as the development of an ever-evolving love.

Billions of years ago, there was only inanimate matter; the ever-evolving love imbedded in it led to the interplay of molecular forces and the breakthrough to life. Where before there were only lifeless minerals and chemical elements interacting, now there were plants, trees, birds and animals.

With the birth of life and the growth of biological things, evolving love was directed toward reproduction and proliferation of plants, animals, birds, fish.

The appearance of humans marked a third stage of evolu-

21. Robert Theobald, *An Alternative Future for America II* (Chicago: Swallow, 1970), p. 44.

tionary love-energy. A spiritual and personal dimension was added. The ever-evolving love that was in the universe from the beginning created richer and richer levels of complexity and depth in relating. Families, communities, and ever-larger groups of friends in dialogue began to evolve.[22]

According to Teilhard de Chardin, the human race is evolving toward a universal friendship.

Many biologists, physicists and ecologists assert that the universe *is* one huge evolving and energized organism. Cosmic friendship means that peole will *realize* this organic unity of all things and fully live its truth.

When that day arrives, everyone will know that they are connected with everyone else. They will experience togetherness at the level of their inner cores.

In the words of philosopher Norman O. Brown, cosmic friendship means

> . . . to find the kingdom in one's own body in the outside world. The body to be realized is the body of the cosmic man, the body of the universe as one perfect man.[23]

For Brown, the one perfect person to be realized will be called "Love," and the body to be realized will be called Love's Body.

Members of One Body

"We are all members of one body," is a fundamental insight of Eastern and Western theologies.

For example, in the East, the concept of the universal self is strong. Various teachings might say, "Thou art the universal self" or "Thou art the Buddha and all things are Buddha things" or "Thine inmost essence is identical with the invisible substance of the all." [24]

22. See Pierre Teilhard de Chardin, *The Phenomenon of Man* (New York: Harper & Row, 1959), pp. 264–268.
23. Norman O. Brown, *Love's Body* (New York: Random House, 1966), p. 226.
24. H. Zimmer, *Philosophies of India* (New York: 1951), p. 149; cf. pp. 309, 361.

In the West, the Christ figure represents the one cosmic body to some people. Paul the apostle asserts to his Roman believers, "We, though many, are one body in Christ, and individually members of one another" (Rom. 12:15).

So Christians experience the sense of one body in Jesus. Mohammedans experience it in Mohammed. The Buddha's followers find their unity symbolized in him. Many blacks feel a sense of oneness with Malcolm X.

Union and unification is totally personal. It is not mere spirits or souls that will come together, but bodies as well. There is *one body* as well as one spirit.

For this to happen, close and third-self friends will learn to be in touch with the universe's highest form of energy—ever-evolving love.

"It is the life-force as well as the ultimate goal toward which the universe is straining and striving," wrote William Johnston describing an insight of mystics about evolving love.[25]

The Not-Yet-Realized

Fidelity to the third self, to the "between-ness," opens friends to the incredible potential of this invisible dimension.

"We only want to show you something we have seen," wrote theologian Paul Tillich, "and to tell you something we have heard."

It is toward universal, cosmic friendship that third-self friendship moves, when it is unhindered by possessiveness or absorption in the other.

In freedom (as opposed to absorption in each other or possessiveness toward each other), friends leave a space for the new, the not-yet-realized.

Daylight

Between many friends, awareness of the possibility of uni-

25. William Johnston, *Silent Music: The Science of Meditation* (New York: Harper & Row, 1974), p. 164.

versal friendship is something yet unconscious that needs to be made conscious. For them, realization of the One Body is a secret to be disclosed, a veil to be rent, a seal to be broken open.

Cosmic awareness, when it comes to a third self, will not be a gradual process, but like every revelation it will break through suddenly.

Old meanings of life, love, friendship will be transformed and reversed.

Symbolic words like "the true bread," "the Ever-Living Fire" "the Inexpressible," "the Way," "Adam," "birth," "heaven," "God," "Tao," "Brahma," "Buddha," and the like, so often verbalized out of habit, will be suddenly understood.

The key for the lock will have been found. Dawn will have broken. Daylight will shine forth from the world's core.

Open the Door

Someone once asked Martin Buber to imagine himself in a situation where he was alone, wholly alone on earth. Then he was offered a choice, either books or humans.

Everyone will correctly guess which choice Buber made, but his response is worth sharing.

> I knew nothing of books when I came forth from the womb of my mother, and I shall die without books, with another human hand in my own. I do, indeed, close my door at times and surrender myself to a book, but only because I can open the door again and see a human being looking at me.[26]

Buber knew, as did Pascal, that "the heart has its reasons that reason does not know."

26. Martin Buber, *Pointing the Way: Collected Essays* (New York: Harper & Row, 1957), p. 4.